VISIONS

Basic Language and Literacy

Caroline Linse

Jane Yedlin

THOMSON
— TM
HEINLE

Australia • Canada • Mexico • Singapore • United Kingdom • United States

VISIONS BASIC STUDENT BOOK
Caroline Linse and Jane Yedlin

Publisher: *Phyllis Dobbins*

Director of Development: *Anita Raducanu*

Senior Developmental Editor and Contributor: *Jill Korey O'Sullivan*

Director, ELL Training and Development: *Evelyn Nelson*

Developmental Editor: *Tania Maundrell-Brown*

Associate Developmental Editor: *Yeny Kim*

Associate Developmental Editor: *Kasia Zagorski*

Editorial Assistant: *Audra Longert*

Production Supervisor: *Mike Burggren*

Marketing Manager: *Jim McDonough*

Manufacturing Manager: *Marcia Locke*

Photography Manager: *Sheri Blaney*

Production Editor: *Samantha Ross*

Design and Production: *Publicom, Inc.*

Cover Designer: *Studio Montage*

Printer: *R.R. Donnelly and Sons Company, Willard*

Cover Image: © *Superstock*

Printed in the United States of America
6 7 8 9 10   08   07   06   05   04

For more information contact Heinle, 25 Thomson Place, Boston, Massachusetts 02210 USA, or you can visit our Internet site at http://www.heinle.com.

For permission to use material from this text or product contact us:
Tel   1-800-730-2214
Fax   1-800-730-2215
Web www.thomsonrights.com

ISBN: 0-8384-0382-4

Reviewers and Consultants

We gratefully acknowledge the contribution of the following educators, consultants, and librarians who reviewed materials at various stages of development. Their input and insight provided us with valuable perspective and ensured the integrity of the entire program.

Program Advisors
Jill Korey O'Sullivan
Evelyn Nelson

Consultants
Deborah Barker
Nimitz High School
Houston, Texas

Sharon Bippus
Labay Middle School
Houston, Texas

Sheralee Connors
Portland, Oregon

Kathleen Fischer
Norwalk LaMirada
   Unified School District
Norwalk, California

Willa Jean Harner
Tiffin-Seneca Public Library
Tiffin, Ohio

Nancy King
Bleyl Middle School
Houston, Texas

Dell Perry
Woodland Middle School
East Point, Georgia

Julie Rines
The Thomas Crane Library
Quincy, Massachusetts

Lynn Silbernagel
The Catlin Gabel School
Portland, Oregon

Cherylyn Smith
Fresno Unified School
   District
Fresno, California

Jennifer Trujillo
Fort Lewis College
Teacher Education
   Department
Durango, Colorado

Teresa Walter
Chollas Elementary School
San Diego, California

Reviewers
Jennifer Alexander
Houston Independent
   School District
Houston, Texas

Susan Alexandre
Trimble Technical
   High School
Fort Worth, Texas

Deborah Almonte
Franklin Middle School
Tampa, Florida

Donna Altes
Silverado Middle School
Napa, California

Ruben Alvarado
Webb Middle School
Austin, Texas

Sheila Alvarez
Robinson Middle School
Plano, Texas

Cally Androtis-Williams
Newcomers High School
Long Island City, New York

Minerva Anzaldua
Martin Middle School
Corpus Christi, Texas

Alicia Arroyos
Eastwood Middle School
El Paso, Texas

Douglas Black
Montwood High School
El Paso, Texas

Jessica Briggeman
International Newcomer
   Academy
Fort Worth, Texas

Diane Buffett
East Side High School
Newark, New Jersey

Eva Chapman
San Jose Unified School
   District Office
San Jose, California

Elia Corona
Memorial Middle School
Pharr, Texas

Alicia Cron
Alamo Middle School
Alamo, Texas

Florence Decker
El Paso Independent
   School District (retired)
El Paso, Texas

Janeece Docal
Bell Multicultural
   Senior High School
Washington, DC

Addea Dontino
Miami-Dade County
   School District
Miami, Florida

Kathy Dwyer
Tomlin Middle School
Plant City, Florida

Olga Figol
Barringer High School
Newark, New Jersey

Claire Forrester
Molina High School
Dallas, Texas

Connie Guerra
Regional Service Center 1
Edinburg, Texas

James Harris
DeLeon Middle School
McAllen, Texas

Audrey Heining-Boynton
University of North
   Carolina-Chapel Hill
School of Education
Chapel Hill, North Carolina

Carolyn Ho
North Harris
   Community College
Houston, Texas

Donald Hoyt
Cooper Middle School
Fresno, California

Nancy A. Humbach
Miami University
Department of Teacher
   Education
Oxford, Ohio

Marie Irwin
University of Texas at
   Arlington Libraries
Arlington, Texas

Mark Irwin
Cary Middle School
Dallas, Texas

Erik Johansen
Oxnard High School
Oxnard, California

Marguerite Joralemon
East Side High School
Newark, New Jersey

Karen Poling Kapeluck
Lacey Instructional Center
Annandale, Virginia

Lorraine Kleinschuster
Intermediate School 10 Q
Long Island City, New York

Fran Lacas
NYC Board of Education
   (retired)
New York, New York

Robert Lamont
Newcomer Center
Arlington, Texas

Mao-ju Catherine Lee
Alief Middle School
Houston, Texas

Leonila Luera
Pharr-San Juan-Alamo ISD
Pharr/San Juan, Texas

Gail Lulek
Safety Harbor Middle School
Safety Harbor, Florida

Natalie Mangini
Serrano International School
Lake Forest, California

Linda Martínez
Dallas Independent
School District
Dallas, Texas

Berta Medrano
Pharr-San Juan-Alamo ISD
Pharr/San Juan, Texas

Graciela Morales
Austin Independent
School District
Austin, Texas

Karen Morante
School District of
Philadelphia
Philadelphia, Pennsylvania

Jacel Morgan
Houston ISD
Houston, Texas

Lorraine Morgan
Hanshaw Middle School
Modesto, California

Dianne Mortensen
Pershing Intermediate
School 220
Brooklyn, New York

Denis O'Leary
Rio del Valle Junior High
School
Oxnard, California

Jeanette Page
School District of
Philadelphia (retired)
Philadelphia, Pennsylvania

Claudia Peréz
Hosler Middle School
Lynwood, California

Yvonne Perez
Alief Middle School
Houston, Texas

Penny Phariss
Plano Independent
School District
Plano, Texas

Bari Ramírez
L. V. Stockard Middle School
Dallas, Texas

Jacqueline Ray
Samuel High School
Dallas, Texas

Howard Riddles
Oak Grove Middle School
Clearwater, Florida

R. C. Rodriguez
Northside Independent
School District
San Antonio, Texas

Randy Soderman
Community School
District Six
New York, New York

Rita LaNell Stahl
Sinagua High School
Flagstaff, Arizona

Dean Stecker
School District of Palm
Beach County
West Palm Beach, Florida

Mary Sterling-Cruz
Jackson Middle School
Friendswood, Texas

Rosemary Tejada
Carlsbad High School
Carlsbad, California

Camille Sloan Telthorster
Bleye Middle School
Houston, Texas

Vickie Thomas
Robinson Middle School
Plano, Texas

Claudio Toledo
Lynwood Middle School
Lynwood, California

Christopher Tracy
Garnet-Patterson Middle
School
Washington, DC

Lydia Villescas
Pharr-San Juan-Alamo ISD
Pharr/San Juan, Texas

Stephanie Vreeland
T.A. Howard Middle
School
Arlington, Texas

Jennifer Zelenitz
Long Island City High
School
Long Island City, New York

We wish to thank the students at the following schools who helped us select high-interest readings at an appropriate language level. Their feedback was invaluable.

Student Reviewers

Cooper Middle School
Fresno, California

De Leon Middle School
McAllen, Texas

Garnet–Patterson Middle
School
Washington, D.C.

Hanshaw Middle School
Modesto, California

Intermediate School 10 Q
Long Island City, New York

Jackson Middle School
Friendswood, Texas

L. V. Stockard Middle
School
Dallas, Texas

Liberty Middle School
Pharr, Texas

Martin Middle School
Corpus Christi, Texas

Memorial Middle School
Pharr, Texas

Newcomer Center
Arlington, Texas

Nimitz High School
Houston, Texas

Oak Grove Middle School
Clearwater, Florida

Oxnard High School
Oxnard, California

Pershing Intermediate
School 220
Brooklyn, New York

Samuel High School
Dallas, Texas

Serrano International School
Lake Forest, California

Silverado Middle School
Napa, California

T. A. Howard Middle
School
Arlington, Texas

Trimble Technical
High School
Fort Worth, Texas

Scope and Sequence

	Letters and Sounds	Language and Vocabulary	Reading And Writing
CHAPTER A **At School** page 2	Consonants: *b, g, m, s, t* Vowel: *a*	Greetings Introductions Mr./Mrs./Miss/Ms.	Introductions
CHAPTER B **In the Classroom** page 14	Consonants: *c, d, f, n, p* Vowel: *o*	*Where are you from?* Countries/Nationalities Numbers 1–10 Colors	The American Flag
CHAPTER C **Classmates** page 28	Consonants: *h, j, l, v, x* Vowels: *i, u*	Clothes Numbers 11–20 Parts of the Body *How old are you?*	Sentences and Questions
CHAPTER D **Around the School** page 40	Consonants: *k, q, r, w, y, z* Vowel: *e*	School Places, Objects, and People Prepositions Asking For and Giving Directions	School Workers

Scope and Sequence

	Vocabulary	Listen, Speak, Interact	Build Vocabulary	Grammar Focus	Word Study	Use Prior Knowledge
CHAPTER 1 **In the School Office** page 52	In the School Office	Making Requests	The Calendar: Days of the Week Months of the Year Ordinal Numbers	Subject Pronouns Possessive Adjectives	Short Vowels: *a, e, i, o, u*	Information About You
CHAPTER 2 **About My Family** page 66	Family Members Pets	Describing People	Adjectives for Describing People	Simple Present Tense of *be* Simple Present Tense of *be*: Negative Contractions with *be*	Long Vowels: *a, i, o, u*	Describe a Baby
CHAPTER 3 **After School** page 80	Activities	Talking About Activities	Sports and Arts Activities	Simple Present	Long *e* Sound: *ee, ea*	Trying Something New
CHAPTER 4 **Home** page 94	Homes Rooms of a Home	Talking About Activities in Different Rooms	Furniture and Objects in Different Rooms of a Home	*There is /* *There are*	Compound Words	Feelings About Home
CHAPTER 5 **The Community** page 108	Community Places and Transportation	Talking About Community Places and Transportation	Time and Schedules	Present Continuous *-ing* Spelling Rules	Digraphs: *ch, sh, th, wh, ng*	Newspapers

Build Background	Text Structure	Reading	Beyond the Reading	From Reading to Writing	Projects
Parents and Guardians	A Form	Student Information Form	Scan for Information	Filling Out a Form Writing Dates Writing Phone Numbers Writing Addresses	Project 1: Make a Class Birthday Book Project 2: Make a Class Calendar
Dimples	Rhyming Poem	"My Baby Brother" by Mary Ann Hoberman	Find Words That Rhyme Shared Reading	Describing a Family Member	Project 1: Family Member Presentation Project 2: Make and Organize Rhyme Cards
Roller Skating	Free Verse Poem	"74th Street" by Myra Cohn Livingston	Organize Pictures Retell the Story Act Out the Poem	Paragraph About a Favorite Activity	Project 1: Activities Collage Project 2: Favorite Activity Presentation
Petunias	Vignette	"A House of My Own" by Sandra Cisneros	Think About the Picture Compare with Words	Paragraph About a Future Home	Project 1: Create Your Dream Home Project 2: Find Compound Nouns
Community Service	Newspaper Article	Newspaper Articles Who / What / When / Where / Why	Scan for Information	Informational Paragraph	Project 1: Make a Transportation Graph Project 2: Create a School Newspaper

Scope and Sequence

	Vocabulary	Listen, Speak, Interact	Build Vocabulary	Grammar Focus	Word Study	Use Prior Knowledge
CHAPTER 6 **Food** page 122	Breakfast, Lunch, and Dinner Foods	Talking About Foods and Diet	Table Settings	Count and Noncount Nouns	Plural Count Nouns: Spelling and Pronunciation	What Foods Are Healthy?
CHAPTER 7 **Money** page 136	Coins and Bills	Talking About Money and Prices	Ways to Pay	Comparative Adjectives	The Prefix *re-*	What Do You Wish For?
CHAPTER 8 **Jobs** page 150	Jobs	Talking About Jobs	Job Tools and Objects	Object Pronouns	The Suffix *-er*	How Do You Order Fast Food?
CHAPTER 9 **Holidays** page 164	Holidays	Talking About Holidays	Holidays Throughout the Year	Past Tense: *be* and Regular Verbs	Consonant Clusters: *s* Blends	Leaders
CHAPTER 10 **Feelings** page 178	Feelings	Talking About Feelings	Verbs Related to Feelings	Future Tense with *will* Future Tense with *will*: Negative Contractions with *will*	Long and Short Vowel Review	Feelings About the First Day of School

Build Background	Text Structure	Reading	Beyond the Reading	From Reading to Writing	Projects
Pyramids	Informational Text	"The Food Guide Pyramid"	Analyze Your Diet Compare Your Diet to the Food Guide Pyramid	Paragraph About Diet Topic Sentence and Details	Project 1: Make a Food Pyramid Poster Project 2: Make a Class Recipe Book
Gold	Myth	"King Midas and the Golden Touch"	Make a Story Timeline Retell the Story	Opinion Paragraph Phrases for Expressing Opinions	Project 1: Make a Menu Project 2: Create a Store
Cash Registers	"How-To" Narration	"How to Take a Fast-Food Order"	Illustrate the Order of Events Retell the Sequence of Events Act Out the Sequence of Events	"How-To" Paragraph Sequence Words	Project 1: Invite a Guest Speaker to Class Project 2: Give a "How-To" Presentation
Peaceful Protest	Biography	"Martin Luther King Jr.: American Leader"	Fill In a Timeline Draw a Picture	Autobiography	Project 1: American Holiday Presentation Project 2: Timeline of a Famous American's Life
Monsters	Poem	"Patti Bennett" by Mel Glenn	Compare and Contrast	Personal Letter Greeting and Closing	Project 1: Keep a Diary Project 2: Act It Out

Learning to read involves a number of different skills. Students must combine knowledge about sounds, letter names, letter shapes, vocabulary, and sentence structure with world knowledge. Learning to read a language with an alphabet, such as English, is different than learning how to read a language written with characters, such as Chinese.

Phonemic Awareness

Learning to read and write an alphabetic language like English is dependent upon the learner's understanding that spoken words are composed of smaller sound units, or phonemes. It is obvious to those of us who already know how to read and write that a word like *book* has three sounds or phonemes: /b/, /oo/, and /k/. Research reveals that many learners do not perceive words as segment-able into separate sound units. This can be particularly true of English language learners (ELLs) who have limited experience listening to standard English speech. However, awareness of the separate phonemes that make up a word is critical for matching those sounds with letters to "sound out" or "decode" a word.

The ability to hear the individual phonemes that compose a word may be developed and enhanced through oral activities that call attention to rhythm, rhyme, alliteration and other sound qualities of words. English language learners who are from environments that are not rich in literacy are among those most likely to benefit greatly from such activities. (Adams, 1998) (Blachman, 2000) (Snow, Burns & Griffin, 1998) (Verhoeven, 1999)

Knowledge of Letter Shapes and Names

Learning to read and write depends upon the ability to visually discriminate one letter from another. Learners must be aware of the features of shape that differentiate written letters (graphemes) such as *o* and *u;* or *m* and *n.* They must also learn to recognize directional orientations that differentiate letters with similar graphic features such as *d* and *b; p* and *q;* or *w* and *m.* As if that were not enough, literacy learners must also learn the one-to-one correspondence between distinctly shaped pairs of uppercase and lowercase letters such as *A* and *a;* or *G* and *g.* Learners who have not been immersed since early childhood in a rich print environment featuring the Roman alphabet may require extensive practice in recognizing and discriminating the 26 letters in their uppercase and lowercase forms.

Moreover, research indicates that the ability to identify letters by name is a strong predictor of learning to read. Letter names provide a system of labels for talking about and classifying graphemes, the symbols that make up words. Letter names provide a bridge from students' recognition of letter shapes to their mapping of sounds onto these shapes. (Adams, 1995) (New Standards Primary Literacy Committee, 1999) (Snow, Burns & Griffin, 1998)

Explicit Phonics Instruction

Explicit phonic instruction teaches the relationships between sounds (phonemes) and the printed letters (graphemes). Students are first taught the sounds made by consonants at the beginnings of words. Then students are taught the sounds of consonants at the ends of words, vowel sounds, and blends. (Pinnel & Fountas, 1998) (Snow, Burns & Griffin, 1998)

Word Identification Skills

Students need to know how to pronounce and understand the printed words that they encounter. Students learn to decode, or sound out words, applying their knowledge of grapheme (letter) / phoneme (sound) correspondence. Other types of skills needed for word identification include: knowledge of word parts such as roots, prefixes, and suffixes; knowledge of the visual configurations of high frequency words that cannot easily be sounded out (*the, he, were*); and knowledge of how to use context clues. (Adams, 1995) (New Standards Primary Literacy Committee, 1999)

Fluency

Reading fluency refers to the ability to read aloud smoothly without frequent or lengthy pauses for word identification. Fluent reading has prosody (phrasing, rhythm, and intonation) appropriate to the meaning. Research supports repeated guided oral reading of texts as the most effective instruction for achieving fluency. Texts that recycle or spiral vocabulary across lessons help students develop fluency and comprehension. (Fountas & Pinnel, 1996) (Hiebert, 1999) (Stahl, Heuback, & Cramond, 1997)

Spelling Instruction

Spelling instruction supports both writing and reading skills, teaching students the various patterns in which letters clustered together form sounds and words. Spelling instruction supports students as they go from being emergent to proficient readers. (Ehri, 1997) (Pinnel, & Fountas, 1998) (Templeton, & Morris, 2000)

Vocabulary Instruction

To support reading comprehension, vocabulary instruction should increase the number of words known and the depth of such knowledge, including multiple meanings for words used in school. New words are best learned in context and in relation to other words. Vocabulary instruction should also teach students word analysis strategies involving prefixes, suffixes, and root words. Vocabulary knowledge involves understanding words in both spoken and written form. Word-learning requires multiple encounters with a word in its various contexts. Research identifies limited vocabulary knowledge as the greatest impediment to reading comprehension among English language learners. Research demonstrates that vocabulary instruction to ELLs can promote gains in word knowledge and in reading comprehension. (Anderson, 1999) (Garcia, 2000) (Blachowitz & Fisher, 2000) (Beck & McKeown, 1991) (Nation, 1990)

Comprehension Strategies

Simply sounding out individual words is not reading. Reading involves making meaning from print. Students can be helped to build reading comprehension in a variety of ways. These include pre-reading activities to elicit, assess, and build on students'

prior knowledge of the topic and vocabulary. Guiding questions give students goals for their reading, and a preview of chapter headings and sections provide a helpful map of what to expect. Teachers can engage students in monitoring comprehension by helping them to paraphrase and summarize chunks of text as they read. Helping students to figure out what is going to happen next or what type of information may be provided next is an example of a simple but effective reading comprehension strategy. (Anderson, 1999) (Carrell, Devine, & Eskey, 1988) (Pressley, 2000) (Pritchard, 1990)

Integration of Listening, Speaking, Reading, and Writing

Language use consists of four distinct skills or modalities, practiced in combination with one another: listening, speaking, reading, and writing. For example, when there is a speaker, there is usually a listener as well. Writers engage readers in interpreting and enjoying their work. Listening and reading are considered receptive skills, and speaking and writing are considered productive skills. Progress in the four skills may be uneven but is inter-related. Good instruction should integrate all four modalities. For example, students could listen to a story, talk about it, read the story or a related story for themselves, and then respond in writing. (Echevarria, Vogt, & Short, 2000) (Ediger, 2001) (Peregoy & Boyle, 1997) (Goldenberg, 1993) (Goldenberg & Pathey-Chavez, 1995)

Learning Strategies

Learning strategies refer to the way that learners successfully tackle different learning tasks such as memorizing a word list, writing a report, or studying for a test. Students who are effective at learning use a variety of strategies to complete their assignments. These strategies include different ways of getting ready to perform a task, actually performing the task, and working with others to complete the task.

References

Adams, M.J. *Beginning to Read: Thinking and Learning about Print.* Cambridge, MA: MIT Press, 1995.

Adams, M.J. "The Elusive Phoneme." *American Educator:* Spring/Summer 1998.

Anderson, N. *Exploring Second Language Reading.* Boston: Heinle and Heinle Publishers, 1999.

Beck, I. and McKeown, M. "Conditions of Vocabulary Learning." Kamil, Mosenthal. Pearson, and Barr (Eds.) *Handbook of Reading Research.* Mahwah, NJ: Lawrence Erlbaum, 2000.

Blachman, B.A. "Phonological Awareness." Kamil, Mosenthal. Pearson, and Barr (Eds.) *Handbook of Reading Research.* Mahwah, NJ: Lawrence Erlbaum, 2000.

Blachowitz, C.L.Z. and Fisher, P. "Vocabulary Instruction" in Kamil, Mosenthal. Pearson, and Barr (Eds.) *Handbook of Reading Research.* Mahwah, NJ: Lawrence Erlbaum, 2000.

Carrell, P., Devine, J.; & Eskey, D. (Eds.) *Interactive approaches to Second Language Reading.* Cambridge, UK: Cambridge University Press, 1998.

Chamot, A.U., Dale, M., O'Malley, J.M., & Spanos, G. "Learning and problem-solving strategies of ESL students." *Bilingual Research Journal* 16 (1992): 133.

Chamot, A.U., & O'Malley, J. *The Calla Handbook.* Reading, MA: Addison-Wesley, 1995.

Echevarria, J.; Vogt, M., Short, D. *Making Content Comprehensible for English Language Learners.* Needham Heights: Allyn & Bacon, 2000.

Ediger, A. "Teaching Children Literacy Skills in a Second Language." Celce-Murcia (Ed.) *Teaching English as a second or foreign language.* Boston, MA: Heinle & Heinle, 2001.

Ehri, L. "Learning to spell and learning to read are one in the same, almost." Perfetti, & Fayol (Eds.) *Learning to spell: research, theory, and practice across languages.* Mahwah, NJ: Lawrence Erlbaum, 2000.

Fountas, I.C. & Pinnel, G.S. *Guided Reading.* Portsmouth, NH: Heinnemann, 1996.

Garcia, G.E. "Bilingual Children's Reading." Kamil, Mosenthal. Pearson, and Barr (Eds.) *Handbook of Reading Research.* Mahwah, NJ: Lawrence Erlbaum, 2000.

Goldenberg, C. "Instructional conversations: Promoting comprehension through discussion." *The Reading Teacher,* 46 (1993): 316–326.

Goldenberg, C. & Pathey-Chavez, G. "Discourse Processes in Instructional Conversations: Interactions Between Teacher and Transition Readers." *Discourse Processes* 19 (1995): 57–74.

Hiebert, E. "Text Matters in Learning to Read." *Reading Teacher* (1999): 552–568.

Nation, P. *Teaching and Learning Vocabulary.* Boston, MA: Heinle & Heinle, 1990.

New Standards Primary Literacy Committee. *Reading and Writing Grade by Grade: Primary Literacy Standards for Kindergarten Through Third Grade.* Pittsburgh, PA: National Center on Education and the Economy, 1999.

Oxford, R. "Language Learning Strategies." *The Cambridge Guide to Teaching English to Speakers of Other Languages.* Cambridge, UK: Cambridge University Press, 2001.

Peregoy, S. & Boyle, O. *Reading, Writing, and Learning in ESL.* White Plains, NY: Longman, 1997.

Pinnel, G.S. and Fountas, I.C., "Word Matters: Teaching Phonics and Spelling." *The Reading/Writing Classroom,* 1998.

Pressley, M. "What should comprehension instruction be the instruction of?" Kamil, Mosenthal. Pearson, and Barr (Eds.) *Handbook of Reading Research.* Mahwah, NJ: Lawrence Erlbaum, 2000.

Pritchard, R. "The effects of cultural schemata in text processing." *Reading Research Quarterly:* 25 (1990): 273–295.

Snow, C.E., Burns, M.S., & Griffin, S. (Eds). *Preventing reading failure in young children.* Washington, DC: National Academy Press, 1998.

Stahl, S.A., Heuback, K., & Cramond, B. *Fluency-oriented Reading Instruction.* National Reading Research Center, 1997.

Templeton, S. and Morris, D. "Spelling. . ." Kamil, Mosenthal. Pearson, and Barr (Eds.) *Handbook of Reading Research.* Mahwah, NJ: Lawrence Erlbaum, 2000.

Verhoeven, L. (1999). "Second language reading." In Wagner, Vanes, & Street (Eds.), *Literacy: An international handbook.* Boulder: Westview Press.

Visions is a language development program that supports students at four levels, from pre-literacy to transition into the mainstream class-room.

Visions: Basic Language and Literacy provides support for students with little or no knowledge of written English. Students progress from letter recognition and formation, phonics/phonemic awareness, vocabulary building, and reading and writing. In **Visions: Language, Literature, Content,** Levels A, B, and C, students learn and practice skills and strategies to meet grade-level standards and achieve academic success.

Components-At-A-Glance

For Students		Basic Book	Book A	Book B	Book C
Student Book	offers accessible, authentic literature with a balance of fiction and non-fiction, including excerpts from novels, short stories, plays, poetry, narratives, biographies, and informational and content-based readings. The Basic Level systematically presents letter formation, sound-symbol relationships, phonics, and phonemic awareness for newcomer students with little or no literacy skills. Vocabulary building as well as reading and writing at the sentence and paragraph level are emphasized.	●	●	●	●
Activity Book	emphasizes reinforcement and practice of standards-based knowledge and highlights state test-taking skills. Basic Level extends opportunity for student practice of basic reading and writing skills, and includes beginning level content readings.	●	●	●	●
Student Handbook	provides helpful summaries of strategies and review material for student reference.	●	●	●	●
Heinle Reading Library	offers 18 soft cover classics tied to the themes of *Visions: Language, Literature, Content,* and designed for student independent reading.		●	●	●
Basic Mini-Readers	are lively, contemporary stories carefully designed so that students practice the sounds, letters, grammar, and vocabulary presented in the text and in new contexts. The mini-readers are contained in each student's Basic Activity Book.	●			
Student CD-ROM	provides an opportunity for interactive practicing, reteaching, and reinforcing of listening/speaking skills, reading skills, and phonics/phonemic awareness.	●	●	●	●
Audio CDs*	feature all reading selections recorded for auditory learning and building listening/speaking skills, and reading fluency.	●	●	●	●
Newbury House Dictionary with CD-ROM	helps students develop essential dictionary and vocabulary-building skills. Features a pronunciation CD-ROM.		●	●	●
Basic Newbury House Dictionary	is designed for beginning-level students to transition from bilingual and picture dictionaries, and provides clear sample sentences, abundant graphics, and activities.	●			
More Grammar Practice Workbook	helps students learn and review essential grammar skills.		●	●	●
Web site **http://visions.heinle.com**	features additional skill-building activities for students.	●	●	●	●

*Also featured on Audio Tape.

For Teachers		Basic Book	Book A	Book B	Book C
Teacher Edition	contains point-of-use lesson suggestions and multi-level activities developed specifically to meet state standard requirements.		●	●	●
Teacher Resource Book	provides easy-to-use-and-implement lesson plans aligned with state standards. Additional support includes graphic organizers to support lesson activities, CNN® video transcripts, Video Worksheets for students, and a summary of each reading in English and translated into Cambodian, Haitian Creole, Hmong, Cantonese, Spanish, and Vietnamese. School-to-Home Newsletters, in English and the six languages, encourage family involvement. Basic Level includes scripts, extensive teaching notes and step-by-step teacher instructions. **Also available on CD-ROM for teacher customization.**	●	●	●	●
Assessment Program	features diagnostic tests and standards-based quizzes, tests, and exams to ensure accountability, with checklists and tracking systems to monitor individual student progress. **Also available on CD-ROM with ExamView® test-generating software, which allows teachers to create customized tests in minutes from a test bank for each chapter.**	●	●	●	●
Transparencies	offer graphic organizers, reading summaries, and grammar charts for interactive teaching. Basic Level transparencies focus on key concepts for literacy-level students.	●	●	●	●
Staff Development Handbook and Video	provide step-by-step training for all teachers.	●	●	●	●
CNN® Video	features thematic news segments from today's headlines to help build content comprehension through meaningful and realistic viewing activities.		●	●	●
Web site http://visions.heinle.com	features additional teaching resources and an opportunity for teachers to share classroom management techniques with an online community.	●	●	●	●

teacher

man

boy

1 🎧 Listen and point. 👂 ✍️

2 🎧 Listen and repeat. 👂 👄

Activity Book
Pages 1–3

school

woman

girl

student

Letters and Sounds

Consonants: b, g, m, s, t   Vowel: a

3 🎧 Listen and repeat. 👂 👄

m    s    t

man   **school**   **teacher**

4 🎧 Listen and repeat. 👂 👄

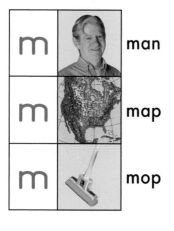

m		man
m		map
m		mop

s		school
s		student
s		sun

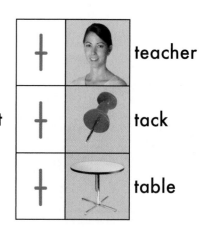

t		teacher
t		tack
t		table

5 Trace.

M M m m S S s s T T t t

VISIONS

Activity Book
Page 4

6 🎧 Listen and repeat. 👂 👄

a   apple

b   boy

g   girl

7 🎧 Listen and repeat. 👂 👄

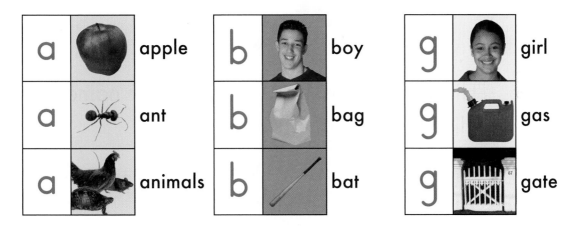

a		apple
a		ant
a		animals

b		boy
b		bag
b		bat

g		girl
g		gas
g		gate

8 Trace.

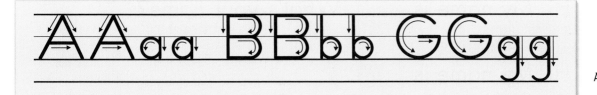

Activity Book
Page 5

AaBbCcDdEeFfGgHhIiJjKkLlMm

Language and Vocabulary

9 🎧 Listen and point.

Hi. My name is Tran. What's your name?

Hi. My name is Ana.

Hi. My name is Lisa. What's your name?

Hi. My name is Emilio.

10 🎧 Listen and repeat.

Tran: Hi. My name is Tran. What's your name?
Ana: Hi. My name is Ana.

Lisa: Hi. My name is Lisa. What's your name?
Emilio: Hi. My name is Emilio.

11 Introduce yourself.

Hi. My name is ___. What's your name?

Hi. My name is ___.

Words to Know

Mr.
Mrs.
Miss
Ms.
hello = hi
Good morning.
Good afternoon.

12  Listen and point.

Good morning. My name is Mrs. Garcia. I'm your teacher.

Hello, Mrs. Garcia. My name is Ana.

13  Listen and repeat.

Mrs. Garcia:	Good morning. My name is Mrs. Garcia. I'm your teacher.
Ana:	Hello, Mrs. Garcia. My name is Ana.

14  Listen and repeat.

 Hello. I'm Mrs. Green.

 Hello. I'm Miss Rana.

 Hi. I'm Mr. Smith.

 Hi. I'm Ms. Allen.

Chapter A At School **7**

Letters and Sounds

Consonants: b, g, m, s, t   Vowel: a

15 🎧 Blend the letter sounds. 👂 ✋ 👄

b ➡ a ➡ t bat   m ➡ a ➡ n man

b ➡ a ➡ g bag   s ➡ a ➡ t sat

g ➡ a ➡ s gas   t ➡ a ➡ g tag

16 Write the letters. ✏️

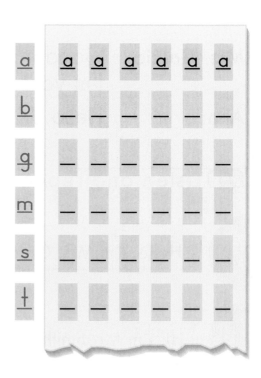

17 Write the words.

1 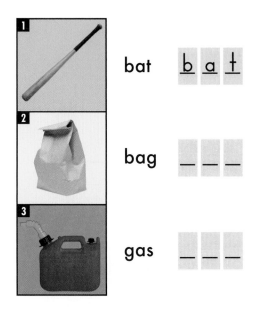 bat <u>b</u> <u>a</u> <u>t</u>

2 bag ___ ___ ___

3 gas ___ ___ ___

4 man ___ ___ ___

5 sat ___ ___ ___

6 tag ___ ___ ___

18 What's the missing letter?

1 b<u>a</u>g

2 sa__

3 __an

4 b__t

5 ta__

6 ga__

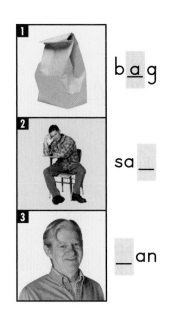
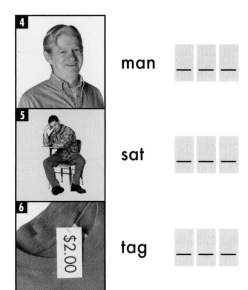
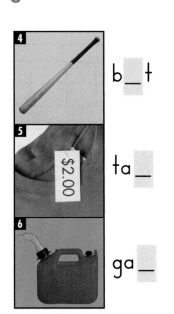

AaBbCcDdEeFfGgHhIiJjKkLlMm

Reading and Writing

19 🎧 Listen and point. 👂 ✍

20 🎧 Listen and repeat. 👂 👄

21 Write the letters. ✍

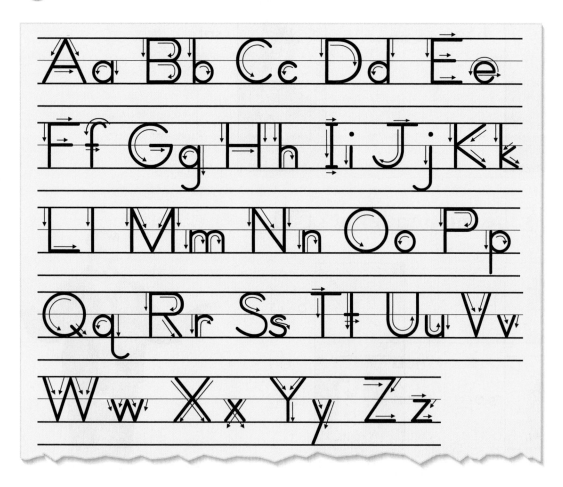

Activity Book
Page 6

NnOoPpQqRrSsTtUuVvWwXxYyZz

22 Point and match.

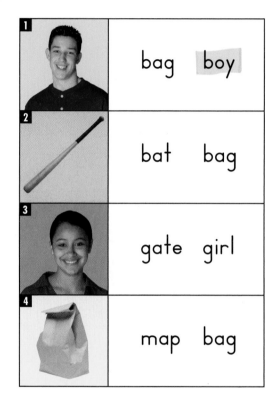

1	bag **boy**
2	bat bag
3	gate girl
4	map bag

5	man map
6	mop map
7	gate tack
8	sat sun

23 Point and match.

1. bag   bat   map   **bag**   boy
2. man   map   man   mop   ant
3. gate   gate   gas   tag   girl
4. map   mop   tag   man   map
5. girl   gate   boy   girl   tack
6. sat   sun   tag   ant   sat

Reading and Writing

24 Read and speak. 📖 👄

A: Good morning. My name is Mrs. Garcia.
I'm your teacher. What's your name?

B: Hello. My name is ___ .

25 Write the words. ✏️

1. my — m y

2. name — _ _ _ _

3. is — _ _

4. what's — _ _ _ _ ' _

5. your — _ _ _ _

26 Write the sentences. ✏️

1. What's your name?

2. My name is _____ .

Activity Book
Pages 7–8

NnOoPpQqRrSsTtUuVvWwXxYyZz

Review

Student
CD-ROM

I can pronounce and spell these words and expressions.

Words

a	I	Mr.	school	your
am	I'm	Mrs.	student	
an	is	Ms.	teacher	
boy	man	my	what's	
girl	Miss	name	woman	

Expressions

Hi.

Hello.

Good morning.

Good afternoon.

My name is ____ .
What's your name?

The Alphabet

Aa Bb Cc Dd Ee Ff Gg Hh Ii Jj Kk Ll Mm

Nn Oo Pp Qq Rr Ss Tt Uu Vv Ww Xx Yy Zz

CHAPTER B

In the Classroom

board

flag

eraser

marker

1 🎧 Listen and point. 👂 ✍️

2 🎧 Listen and repeat. 👂 👄

VISIONS
Activity Book
Page 9

pencil

notebook

backpack

desk

classroom

window

clock

door

pen

computer

chair

book

Letters and Sounds

Consonants: c, d, f, n, p   Vowel: o

3 🎧 Listen and repeat. 👂 👄

c computer

d desk

f flag

4 🎧 Listen and repeat. 👂 👄

c	computer	d	desk	f	flag
c	cap	d	door	f	foot
c	cat	d	dog	f	fan

5 Point to the beginning letter. ✋

 d c s

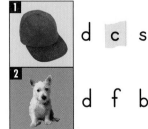 d f b

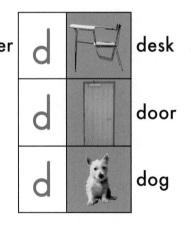 d b f

 m s c

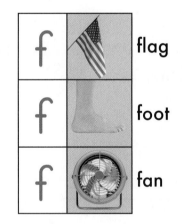 b g d

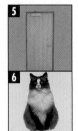 c t a

6 🎧 Listen and repeat. 👂 👄

notebook   office   pencil

7 🎧 Listen and repeat. 👂 👄

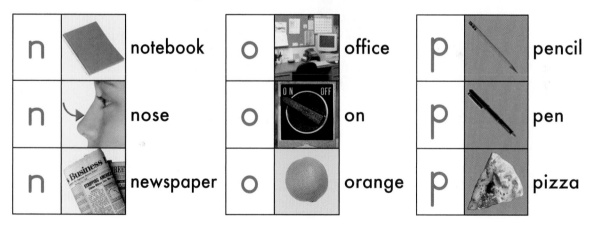

n		notebook	o		office	p		pencil
n		nose	o		on	p		pen
n		newspaper	o		orange	p		pizza

8 Point to the beginning letter. ✍

1   n m o

2   a o f

3   p b g

4   a c o

5   m n c

6   p g b

VISIONS
Activity Book
Page 10

Language and Vocabulary

9 🎧 Listen and point. 👂 🤝

I'm Tran.
I'm from Vietnam.

My name is Pablo.
I'm Colombian.
Where are you from?

I'm Irina. I'm from Russia.

10 🎧 Listen and repeat. 👂 👄

Tran: I'm Tran.
I'm from Vietnam.

Pablo: My name is Pablo.
I'm Colombian.
Where are you from?

Irina: I'm Irina. I'm from Russia.

NnOoPpQqRrSsTtUuVvWwXxYyZz

11 🎧 Listen and repeat. 👂 👄

Country		Nationality
Brazil		Brazilian
China		Chinese
Colombia		Colombian
Cuba		Cuban
Guatemala		Guatemalan
Haiti		Haitian
Mexico		Mexican
Russia		Russian
United States		American
Vietnam		Vietnamese

12 Work with a partner. 👄 👂

A: I'm (name) . I'm from (country) .
Where are you from?

B: I'm (name) . I'm (nationality) .

Activity Book
Pages 11–12

Letters and Sounds

Consonants: c, d, f, n, p   Vowel: o

13 🎧 Blend the letter sounds. 👂 ✍️ 👄

c ➡ a ➡ t   cat   d ➡ o ➡ t   dot

f ➡ a ➡ n   fan   p ➡ o ➡ t   pot

n ➡ a ➡ p   nap   d ➡ o ➡ g   dog

14 What's the missing letter? ✍️

d <u>o</u> g

_ an

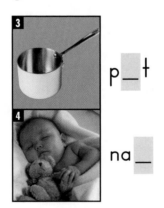

p _ t

na _

15 Say the words. 👄

1. dog   **2.** fan   **3.** pot   **4.** cat   **5.** nap

16 Write the words. 📝

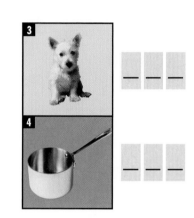

1. f a n

2. _ _ _

3. _ _ _

4. _ _ _

17 🎧 Spell the words. 👂 📝

1. n a p

2. _ _ _

3. _ _ _

4. _ _ _

18 Find the words. 📝

1. n a f   f a n

2. a g b   _ _ _

3. a n m   _ _ _

4. t a c   _ _ _

5. a g t   _ _ _

VISIONS

Activity Book
Page 13

AaBbCcDdEeFfGgHhIiJjKkLlMm

Reading and Writing

19 View and match.

1 door desk
2 bag flag

3 desk book
4 flag foot

20 Listen and read.

My name is Mrs. Garcia. I'm a teacher. This is my classroom. This is my desk.

Hi. I'm Ana. I'm from Mexico. I'm a student. That is my school.

Hi. My name is Lisa. I'm a student. I'm American.

21 Write about yourself.

1. My name is _____. **2.** I'm from _____.

Words to Know

thirteen = 13
fifty = 50
square = ☐

22 🎧 Listen and read. 🔊 📖

The American Flag

This is the American flag.
It is red, white, and blue.
It has thirteen stripes and fifty stars.
The stripes are red and white.
The stars are white on a square of blue.
What does this flag mean to you?

23 What are the missing words? ✍️

1. This is the American f l a g .

2. It is red, white, and _ _ _ _ .

3. It has thirteen stripes and fifty _ _ _ _ _ .

4. The stripes are _ _ _ and white.

Language and Vocabulary

24 🎧 Listen and repeat. 👂 👄

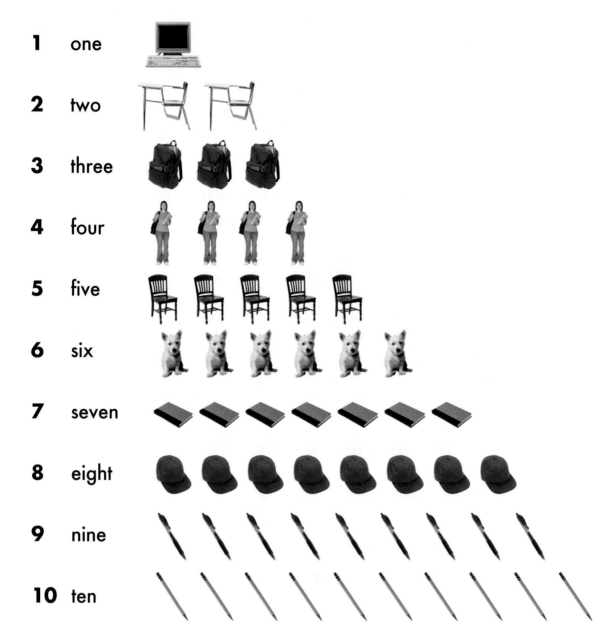

1 one

2 two

3 three

4 four

5 five

6 six

7 seven

8 eight

9 nine

10 ten

25 Trace the numbers.

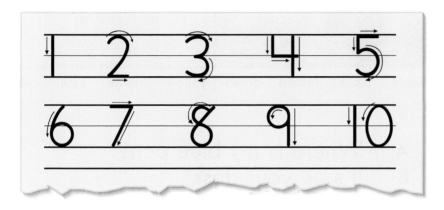

26 What are the missing numbers?

1   2   3   4   _   6   _   8   _   10

27 What are the missing letters?

1. o n e   **3.** _ hr _ _   **5.** _ iv _

2. _ w _   **4.** f _ _ r

AaBbCcDdEeFfGgHhIiJjKkLlMm

Language and Vocabulary

28 🎧 Listen and repeat. 👂👄

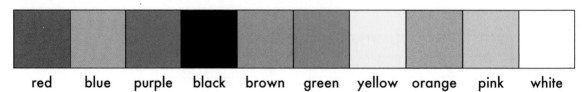

red   blue   purple   black   brown   green   yellow   orange   pink   white

1.   **A:**   Where is my blue pen?
      B: It's on your desk.

2.   **A:**   Where is your green backpack?
      B: It's under my chair.

3.   **A:**   Is this your black pen?
      B: Yes, it is.

4.   **A:**   Where is your red notebook?
      B: It's in my backpack.

5.   **A:**   Where is the pink marker?
      B: It's on the desk.

6.   **A:**   Is that my yellow pencil?
      B: No, it isn't.

Activity Book
Page 16

NnOoPpQqRrSsTtUuVvWwXxYyZz

Review

Student
CD-ROM

I can spell and pronounce these words and expressions.

Words

and	clock	in	pen	under
are	computer	isn't	pencil	where
backpack	desk	it's	stars	window
board	door	marker	stripes	yes
book	eraser	no	that	you
chair	flag	notebook	the	
classroom	from	on	this	

Colors

black	brown	orange	purple	white
blue	green	pink	red	yellow

Numbers

1 one **3** three **5** five **7** seven **9** nine

2 two **4** four **6** six **8** eight **10** ten

Expressions

Where are you from?

I'm from (country) .

I'm (nationality) .

CHAPTER C

Classmates

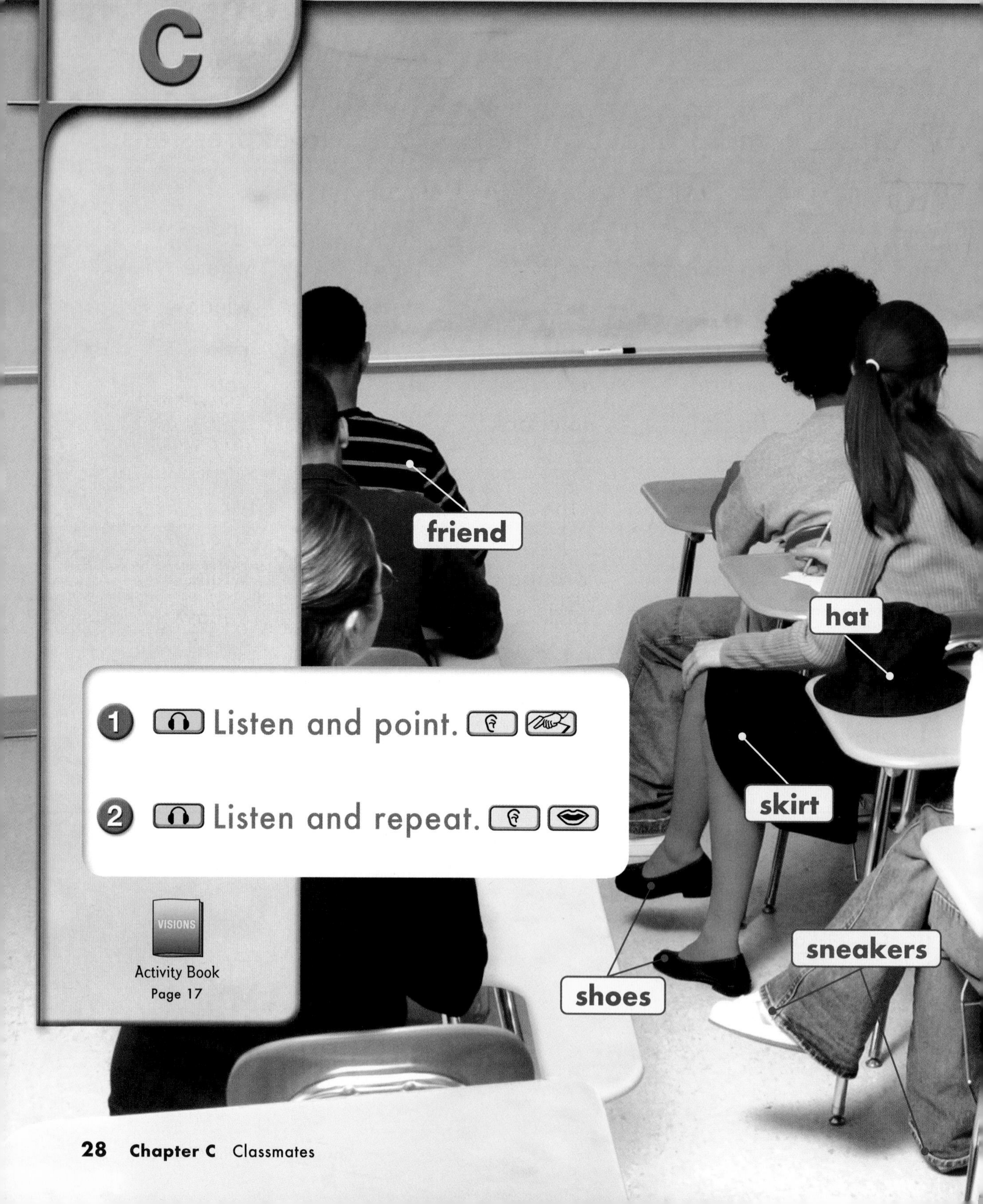

friend
hat
skirt
shoes
sneakers

1 Listen and point.

2 Listen and repeat.

Activity Book
Page 17

He is a student.

sweater

classmates

jacket

shirt

jeans

Letters and Sounds

Consonants: h, j, l, v, x   Vowels: i, u

3 🎧 Listen and repeat. 👂 👄

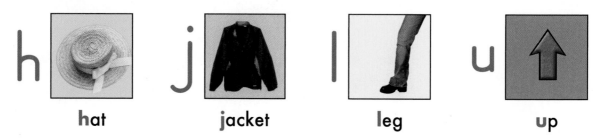

h **hat**   j **jacket**   l **leg**   u **up**

4 🎧 Listen and repeat. 👂 👄

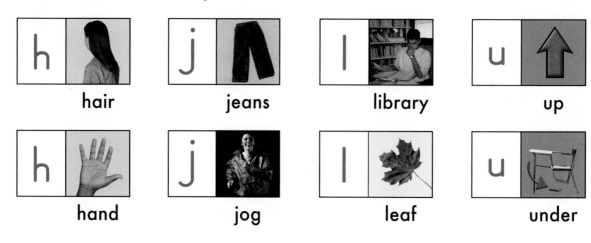

h **hair**   j **jeans**   l **library**   u **up**

h **hand**   j **jog**   l **leaf**   u **under**

5 Point to the beginning letter. 👆

1   h j l
2   j h l
3   l j h
4   l h j
5   j l h
6   h l j

6 🎧 Listen and repeat. 👂 👄

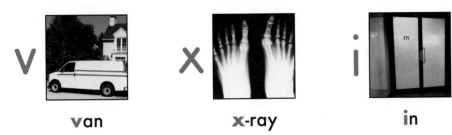

van   x-ray   in

7 🎧 Listen and repeat. 👂 👄

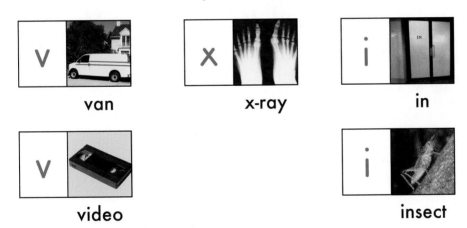

van   x-ray   in

video   insect

8 Point to the beginning letter. 👉

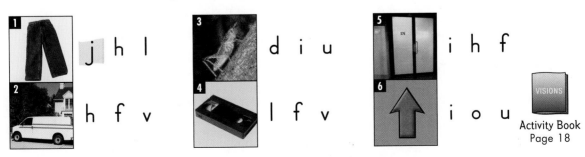

1 j h l

2 h f v

3 d i u

4 l f v

5 i h f

6 i o u

VISIONS
Activity Book
Page 18

AaBbCcDdEeFfGgHhIiJjKkLlMm

Language and Vocabulary

9 🎧 Listen and repeat. 👂 👄

Linda:	Hi. My name is Linda.
Speaker:	How old are you?
Linda:	I'm 15 years old.

Linda | Irina | Emilio

Linda:	These are my friends. Irina is Russian.
Speaker:	How old is Irina?
Linda:	She's 14 years old.

Linda:	Emilio is my friend, too. He's from Mexico.
Speaker:	How old is Emilio?
Linda:	He's 14 years old.

10 🎧 Listen and repeat. 👂 👄

11 eleven ●●●●●●●●●●●●
12 twelve ●●●●●●●●●●●●●
13 thirteen ●●●●●●●●●●●●●●
14 fourteen ●●●●●●●●●●●●●●
15 fifteen ●●●●●●●●●●●●●●●
16 sixteen ●●●●●●●●●●●●●●●●
17 seventeen ●●●●●●●●●●●●●●●●●
18 eighteen ●●●●●●●●●●●●●●●●●●
19 nineteen ●●●●●●●●●●●●●●●●●●●
20 twenty ●●●●●●●●●●●●●●●●●●●●

VISIONS

Activity Book
Pages 19–20

11 🎧 Listen and repeat. 👂 👄

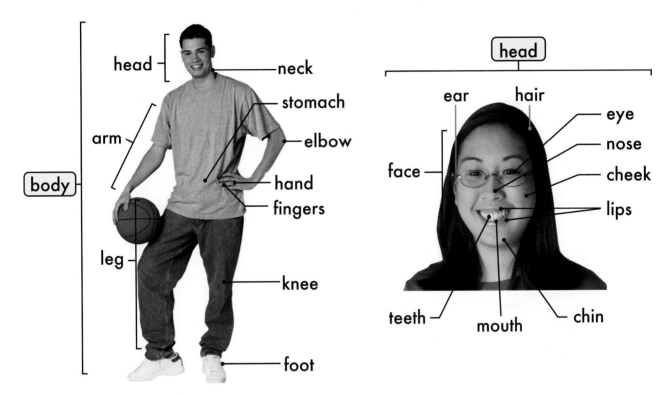

12 Work with a partner. 👄 👂

A: What color is your hair?

B: My hair is ____ .

A: What color are my eyes?

B: Your eyes are ____ .

A: Point to your nose.

B: This is my nose.

Activity Book
Page 21

Letters and Sounds

Consonants: h, j, l, v, x   Vowels: i, u

13 🎧 Blend the letter sounds. 👂 👄

v ➡ a ➡ n   van   s ➡ i ➡ x   six

j ➡ o ➡ g   jog   h ➡ u ➡ g   hug

l ➡ i ➡ p   lip   c ➡ u ➡ p   cup

14 What's the missing letter? 🖊

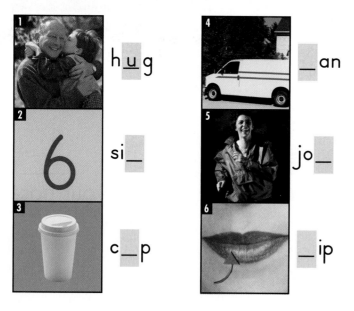

1 h u̲ g

2 si_

3 c_p

4 _an

5 jo_

6 _ip

15 Say the words. 👄

1. six   **2.** van   **3.** jog   **4.** hug   **5.** cup

16 Write the words.

1. jog j o g

2. hug ___

3. six ___

4. van ___

5. cup ___

6. lip ___

17 Spell the words.

1. v a n

2. ___

3. ___

4. ___

18 Is the beginning sound the same?

1. same/different

4. same/different

2. same/different

5. same/different

3. same/different

Activity Book
Page 22

Reading and Writing

19 Read and match.

1. hug	flag	cup	hug	bag
2. jeans	jeans	jog	gas	gate
3. van	fan	tag	man	van
4. cup	map	cat	tag	cup
5. jog	dog	gas	jeans	jog
6. up	hug	up	pen	cup

20 Listen and read.

This is Martha. She is a student. She is 14 years old. Her hair is brown. Her eyes are blue. She is my friend. Is she your friend, too?

NnOoPpQqRrSsTtUuVvWwXxYyZz

21 What are the missing words?

This ___ Emilio. He is ___ student.

He ___ 14 years old. His ___ is black.

His eyes ___ brown. He is ___ friend.

22 Listen and read.

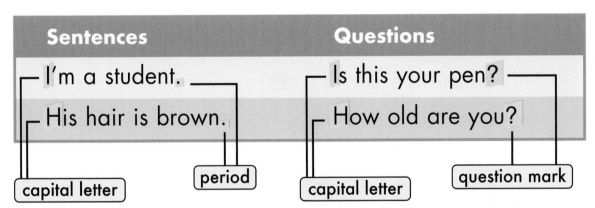

Sentences	Questions
I'm a student.	Is this your pen?
His hair is brown.	How old are you?

capital letter — period — capital letter — question mark

23 Add the punctuation.

1. What's your name ?

2. My name is Ana _

3. _ here are you from?

4. I'm from Mexico _

5. How old is Irina _

6. She is 14 _

VISIONS

Activity Book
Page 23

Language and Vocabulary

24 Listen and repeat.

> A: How many girls are there in this class?
>
> B: There are 14 girls in this class.
>   How many girls are there in your class?
>
> A: There are 11 girls in my class.
>   There are 13 boys.
>
> B: How many teachers are there?
>
> A: There is one teacher.

25 Talk about the picture.

> **Example:** There is a blue backpack. It is under
>   a desk. There are two windows.

Activity Book
Page 24

NnOoPpQqRrSsTtUuVvWwXxYyZz

Review

Student
CD-ROM

I can spell and pronounce these words and expressions.

Words

classmates	her	period	sentence	these
friends	he's	question	she	too
he	his	question mark	she's	

Clothing

hat	jeans	shoes	sneakers
jacket	shirt	skirt	sweater

Numbers

11 eleven	**14** fourteen	**17** seventeen	**19** nineteen
12 twelve	**15** fifteen	**18** eighteen	**20** twenty
13 thirteen	**16** sixteen		

Parts of the body

arm	elbow	hair	lips	teeth
body	eye	hand	mouth	
cheek	face	head	neck	
chin	fingers	knee	nose	
ear	foot	leg	stomach	

Expressions

How old are you?

I'm 13 years old.

How many are there?

There are ____ .

Around the School

cafeteria

gym

1 Listen and point.

2 Listen and repeat.

VISIONS

Activity Book
Page 25

library

librarian

bookcase

bookshelf

hall

locker

bulletin board

stairs

Letters and Sounds

Consonants: k, q, r, w, y, z   Vowel: e

3 🎧 Listen and repeat. 👂 👄

key   ring   window

4 🎧 Listen and repeat. 👂 👄

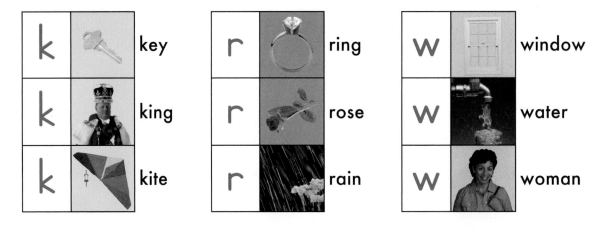

k		key
k		king
k		kite

r		ring
r		rose
r		rain

w		window
w		water
w		woman

5 Point to the beginning letter. ✍

1   k   w   r   3   w   k   r   5   k   r   w

2   r   k   w   4   r   w   k   6   w   r   k

6 🎧 Listen and repeat. 👂 👄

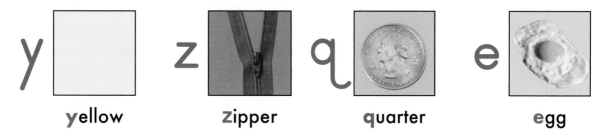

| yellow | zipper | quarter | egg |

7 🎧 Listen and repeat. 👂 👄

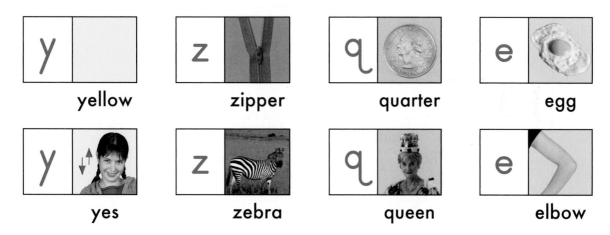

| yellow | zipper | quarter | egg |
| yes | zebra | queen | elbow |

8 Point to the beginning letter. 👆

1   e o u   3   s z x   5   l k t

2   g j y   4   r l n   6   j g q

VISIONS
Activity Book
Page 26

Language and Vocabulary

Words to Know

on the left ⬅
on the right ➡
next to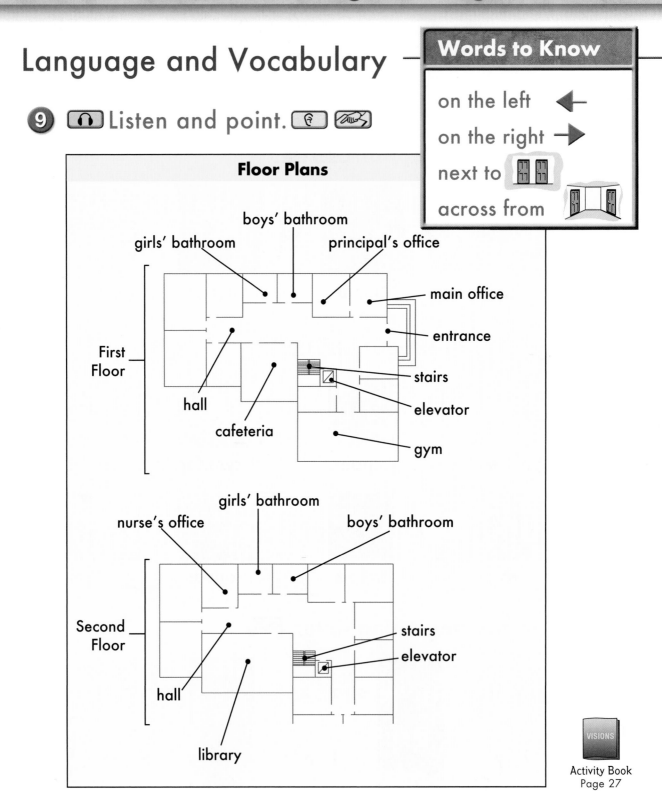
across from

9 🎧 Listen and point. 👂 👆

Floor Plans

boys' bathroom
girls' bathroom
principal's office
main office
entrance
First Floor
stairs
elevator
hall
cafeteria
gym

nurse's office
girls' bathroom
boys' bathroom
Second Floor
stairs
elevator
hall
library

VISIONS

Activity Book
Page 27

10  Listen and repeat.

Words to Know

thanks = thank you
where's = where is

Excuse me.
Where's the gym?

Thanks.

It's on the left. It's
next to Room 102.

Excuse me. Where's
the nurse's office?

It's on the second floor. Go
up the stairs. It's on the left.
It's next to the bathrooms.

Thanks.

11 Answer the questions about your school.

1. Is the nurse's office on the first floor?
2. Is the cafeteria next to the gym?
3. Is the gym on the first floor or the second floor?
4. Where is the library?
5. Where is the main office?
6. What is across from the main office?

VISIONS

Activity Book
Page 28

Letters and Sounds

Consonants: k, q, r, w, y, z   Vowel: e

12 🎧 Blend the letter sounds. 👂 👄

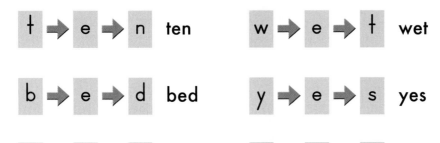

t → e → n   ten   w → e → t   wet

b → e → d   bed   y → e → s   yes

j → e → t   jet   r → e → d   red

13 What's the missing letter? ✏️

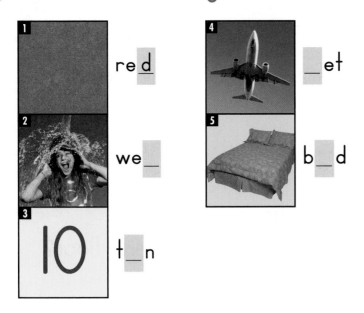

1   re<u>d</u>

4   __et

2   we__

5   b__d

3   10   t__n

14 Say the words.

1. wet   **2.** jet   **3.** red   **4.** bed   **5.** ten   **6.** yes

15 Write the words.

jet   j e t

red   __ __ __

bed   __ __ __

ten   __ __ __

wet   __ __ __

16 Spell the words.

1. j e t   **3.** __ __ __

2. __ __ __   **4.** __ __ __

Activity Book
Page 29

Reading and Writing

17 Read and match. 📖 ✍️

1. y   q   y   g   q   y   p   h

2. z   z   s   w   s   z   z   r

3. q   p   q   g   g   q   y   q

4. k   t   d   t   b   l   k   f

5. r   s   p   r   e   z   n   r

6. w   m   n   w   z   w   n   m

18 Read and match. 📖 ✍️

1.	office	office	room	nice	orange
2.	nurse	nose	rain	rose	nurse
3.	gym	you	my	gym	girl
4.	teacher	table	teacher	student	woman
5.	floor	foot	floor	flag	door
6.	left	left	leg	foot	light
7.	bed	bed	red	boy	bad
8.	name	same	man	note	name

NnOoPpQqRrSsTtUuVvWwXxYyZz

19 🎧 Listen and read. 🔊 📖

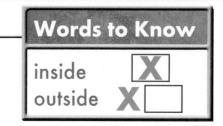

Words to Know

| inside | ☒ |
| outside | ☒ ☐ |

I'm Ms. Fernandez. I'm the principal. This is my office. It's on the first floor. My office is inside the main office. The main office is next to the entrance.

I'm Mr. Soto. I'm the gym teacher. This is the gym. It's on the first floor. The gym is on the left of the main entrance. It's next to Room 102.

My name is Mrs. Walsh. I'm the school nurse. My office is on the second floor. It's across from the library. It's a nice office. There's a desk for me and a bed for sick students.

20 Answer the questions. ✍️

1. Mrs. Walsh is the `nurse` .

2. Mr. Soto is the ___ .

3. The gym is next to ___ 102.

4. The nurse's office is across from the ___ .

VISIONS

Activity Book
Page 30

Language and Vocabulary

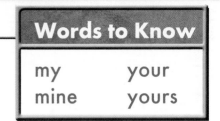

Words to Know

my	your
mine	yours

21  Listen and repeat.

A: Excuse me. Is this the Lost and Found?

B: Yes, it is.

A: I lost my backpack. Maybe it's here.

B: Is this your backpack?

A: No, it isn't. Mine is green.

B: Is this yours?

A: Yes, that's mine. Thank you.

22 What are the missing words?

1. A: Is this your backpack?

   B: No, ___ isn't. Mine ___ red.

2. A: Is this ___ jacket?

   B: ___, it isn't. ___ is black.

3. A: Is this ___ baseball cap?

   B: Yes, it ___. Thank ___.

Activity Book
Page 31–32

NnOoPpQqRrSsTtUuVvWwXxYyZz

Review

Student CD-ROM

I can spell and pronounce these words and expressions.

Words

bathroom	first	library	outside
bookcase	go	locker	principal
bookshelf	gym	main office	second
bulletin board	hall	me	stairs
cafeteria	inside	mine	yours
elevator	librarian	nurse	

Expressions

across from	first floor	on the left	second floor
Excuse me.	next to	on the right	Thank you.

CHAPTER 1

In the School Office

Objectives

Listening and Speaking asking for and giving information

Grammar subject pronouns, possessive adjectives

Word Study short vowels

Reading Student Information Form

Writing filling out a form

Content Activity Book: social studies

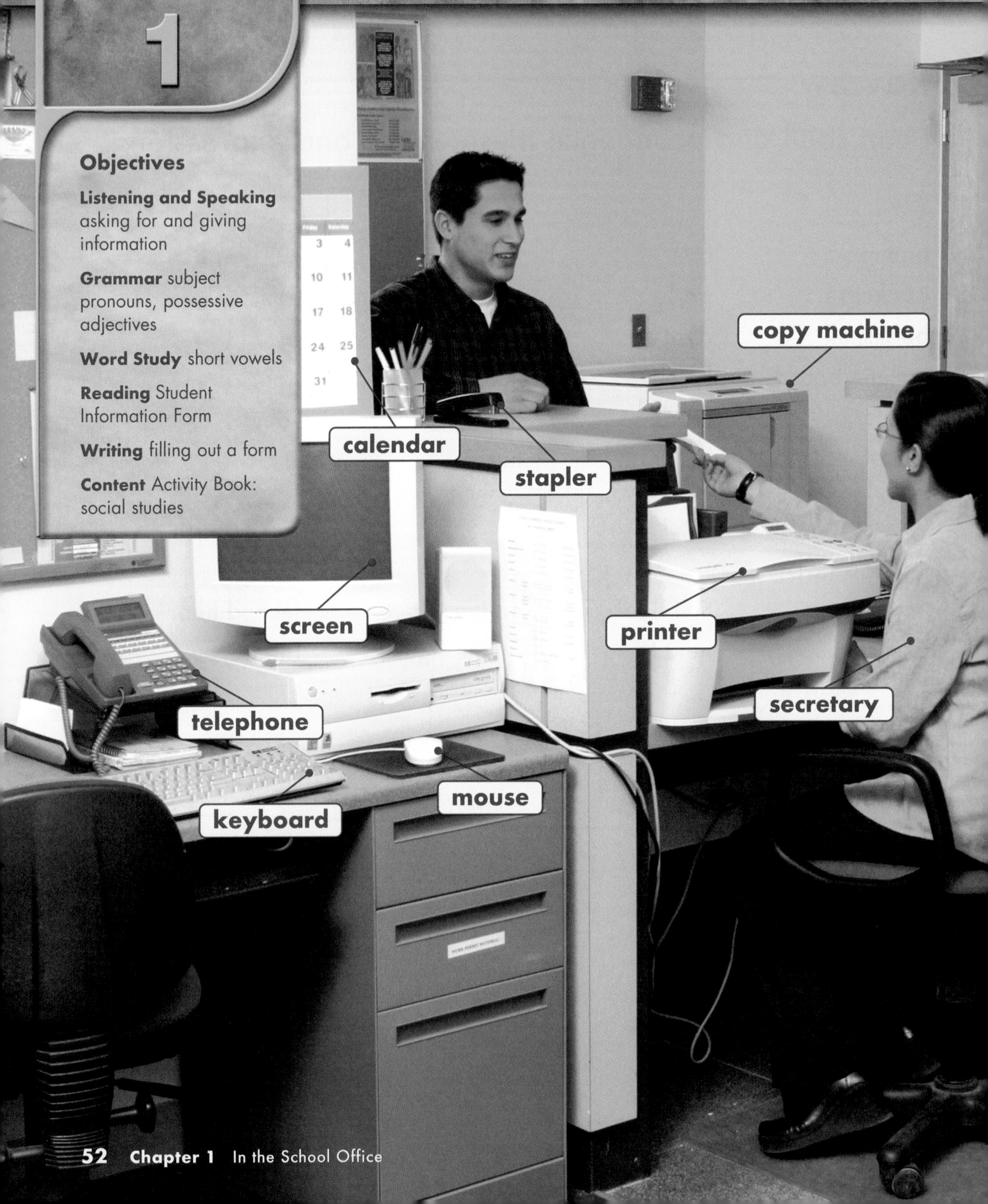

copy machine
calendar
stapler
screen
printer
telephone
secretary
mouse
keyboard

Listen, Speak, Interact

In the School Office

1 🎧 **Listen and repeat.** Listen and repeat the words.

2 🎧 **Listen and repeat.** Listen to the conversation.
Then repeat the conversation.

Secretary:	Good morning. May I help you?
Student:	Yes, please. I need a Student Information Form.
Secretary:	Sure. Here's a Student Information Form.
Student:	Thank you.

3 **Pair work.** Practice the conversation with a partner.

Secretary:	Good morning. May I help you?
Student:	Yes, please. I need a ____ .
Secretary:	Sure. Here's a ____ .
Student:	Thank you.

Build Vocabulary

The Calendar

4 🎧 **Listen and repeat.** Listen and repeat the days of the week.

Sunday	Tuesday	Thursday	Saturday
Monday	Wednesday	Friday	

5 🎧 **Listen and repeat.** Listen and repeat the months.

January	April	July	October
February	May	August	November
March	June	September	December

6 🎧 **Listen and point.** Listen to the dates on the calendar. Point to each date as you hear it.

JANUARY						
Sunday	**Monday**	**Tuesday**	**Wednesday**	**Thursday**	**Friday**	**Saturday**
				1 first	**2** second	**3** third
4 fourth	**5** fifth	**6** sixth	**7** seventh	**8** eighth	**9** ninth	**10** tenth
11 eleventh	**12** twelfth	**13** thirteenth	**14** fourteenth	**15** fifteenth	**16** sixteenth	**17** seventeenth
18 eighteenth	**19** nineteenth	**20** twentieth	**21** twenty-first	**22** twenty-second	**23** twenty-third	**24** twenty-fourth
25 twenty-fifth	**26** twenty-sixth	**27** twenty-seventh	**28** twenty-eighth	**29** twenty-ninth	**30** thirtieth	**31** thirty-first

7 **Pair work.** Say a date on the calendar. Your partner points to the date you say. Take turns.

Activity Book
Page 33

Grammar Focus

Subject Pronouns and Possessive Adjectives

Subject Pronouns	Possessive Adjectives
I am a student.	**My** name is Mario.
You are a secretary.	**Your** stapler is on the desk.
He is from Mexico.	**His** class is in Room 201.
She is 15.	**Her** birthday is in March.
It is here.	**Its** name is Spot.
We are students.	**Our** teacher is in the cafeteria.
They are in the library.	**Their** books are in the backpack.

8 Read and find. Find the subject pronouns in the letter. Then find the possessive adjectives.

9 Choose. Which is the right word?

1. Mario is (I / my) friend.
2. (She / Her) is new at school.
3. (You / Your) pen is on the floor.
4. (They / Their) are from Colombia.
5. (We / Our) class is in Room 311.
6. He is (we / our) teacher.

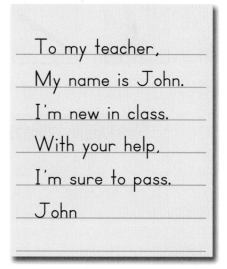

To my teacher,
My name is John.
I'm new in class.
With your help,
I'm sure to pass.
John

Activity Book
Pages 34–35

Word Study

Short Vowels

Short Vowels	
Short a:	bag, cap, man, map
Short e:	yes, bet, wet, ten
Short i:	his, hit, sit, pin
Short o:	hot, job, mop, jog
Short u:	bus, bun, gum, hug

10 🎧 **Listen and repeat.** Listen to the short vowel. Then listen to the short vowel in each word. Repeat each word.

11 **Group work.** Look at the pictures. Say the word for each picture. Copy the chart. Put the words in the correct columns.

Short a	Short e	Short i	Short o	Short u
	egg			

VISIONS
Activity Book
Page 36

Into the Reading

Strategy

Use Prior Knowledge
Before you read about something, think about what you already know. This will help you understand the reading.

You will read a Student Information Form. Students fill out these forms with the information their school needs.

Use Prior Knowledge: Information About You

What information does your school need? Copy the word web on a piece of paper. Fill it in with a partner.

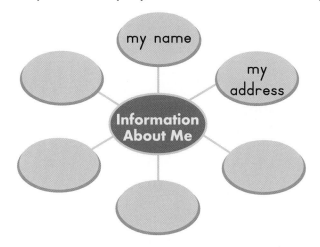

Build Background: Parents and Guardians

Most Student Information Forms ask for the name of your parent or guardian. Your parent is your mother or father. Some students live with another person. This person is called a guardian. What is the name of your parent or guardian?

Reading and Understanding

Text Structure: Form

A form is a piece of paper that has blank spaces. You fill in the blank spaces with information. Different forms ask for different information. Many forms ask for a person's name, address, and phone number.

Reading

STUDENT INFORMATION FORM

DATE: 9/6/04	**GRADE:** 8

LAST NAME: Vega   **FIRST NAME:** Ana   **MIDDLE NAME:** Luisa

ADDRESS

STREET: 1450 West Street

CITY: Los Angeles   **STATE:** California

ZIP CODE: 90022   **PHONE:** (213) 555-1945

DATE OF BIRTH: 8/13/90

PARENT OR GUARDIAN: Miriam Vega

ADDRESS: same address

DAYTIME PHONE: (213) 555-7722

Beyond the Reading

Reading comprehension. Answer the questions.

1. Is Ana a student?

2. What is Ana's date of birth?

3. Is Ana in the seventh grade or the eighth grade?

4. Where does Ana live?

Scan for information. Look at the form again.
Don't read every word. Scan the form for
this information:

- Ana's last name
- Ana's phone number
- Ana's zip code
- Ana's parent or guardian

> **Strategy**
>
> Scan for Information
> To *scan* means to
> read quickly. You
> don't read every
> word. You only
> look for important
> information.

Activity Book
Pages 37–38

From Reading to Writing

Filling Out a Form

Writing dates

1. A date has the month, the day, and the year.
There are two ways to write the date.

2. Write today's date on a piece of paper.
Write the date in two ways.

Writing phone numbers

1. A telephone number includes an
area code and seven numbers.

2. Write your phone number on a piece of paper.

Writing addresses

1. An address has a house or building number, a street,
a city, a state, and a zip code.

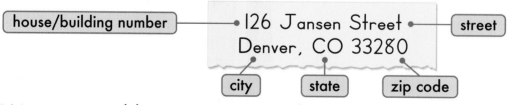

2. Write your address on a piece of paper.

Activity Book
Page 39

Copy the form on a piece of paper. Fill out the form with your own information.

STUDENT INFORMATION FORM

DATE: _____ GRADE: _____

LAST NAME: _____ FIRST NAME: _____ MIDDLE NAME: _____

ADDRESS

STREET: _____

CITY: _____ STATE: _____

ZIP CODE: _____ PHONE: _____

DATE OF BIRTH: _____

PARENT OR GUARDIAN: _____

ADDRESS: _____

DAYTIME PHONE: _____

Editing Checklist

☐ All dates have a month, a day, and a year.

☐ All phone numbers have an area code.

☐ The address has a number, street, city, state, and zip code.

Activity Book
Page 40

Review

Student
CD-ROM

VOCABULARY I can read and spell these words.

address	day	mouse	screen	week
calendar	guardian	parent	secretary	year
copy machine	keyboard	phone number	stapler	zip code
date	month	printer	telephone	

Days of the week
Sunday	Tuesday	Thursday	Saturday
Monday	Wednesday	Friday	

Months of the year
January	April	July	October
February	May	August	November
March	June	September	December

Ordinal numbers
first	fourth	seventh	tenth	thirteenth
second	fifth	eighth	eleventh	fourteenth
third	sixth	ninth	twelfth	fifteenth

Expressions
May I help you?   I need a ____ .   Sure.

GRAMMAR I can use this grammar.
Subject Pronouns and Possessive Adjectives
Subject Pronouns: I, you, he, she, it, we, they
Possessive Adjectives: my, your, his, her, its, our, their

WORD STUDY I can pronounce these short vowels.
Short Vowels
short a: man   **short e:** pen   **short i:** lip   **short o:** hot   **short u:** bus

Assess

VOCABULARY

1. The first month of the year is ____ .

    a. March   **b.** December   **c.** January   **d.** May

Review pages 52–54.

2. There are seven days in a ____ .

    a. year   **b.** week   **c.** month   **d.** Saturday

3. My computer has a screen, a mouse, and a _____ .

    a. telephone   **b.** street   **c.** keyboard   **d.** stapler

GRAMMAR

1. ____ is from Russia.

    a. She   **b.** Her

Review page 55.

2. You are ____ teacher.

    a. I   **b.** my

3. ____ are students.

    a. Their   **b.** They

WORD STUDY What is the vowel sound?

1.

    a. short a
    b. short e
    c. short i
    d. short o

2.

    a. short a
    b. short e
    c. short o
    d. short u

Review page 56.

Projects

Project 1: Make a Class Birthday Book

Work with your class. Make a class birthday book.

1. Write your name and birthday on a piece of paper.
2. Your teacher will collect all of the names. Help put the names in the order of the alphabet.
3. Make a page for the letter A. Write the names of the students with a last name that begins with the letter A. Write their birthdays under their names.
4. Make a new page for each letter of the alphabet. Put the pages together. Add a front cover. Write your room number on the cover. Write your teacher's name. Decorate the cover.

S

Sandoval, Marta
May 5

Sikorsky, Olga
August 17

T

Tang, Carol
February 12

Torres, Diego
September 3

Project 2: Make a Class Calendar

Work with a small group. Make a page of a calendar.

1. Look at a calendar in your class or school office. Choose a month. Draw an empty calendar page on a piece of poster paper.
2. Write the name of the month on the calendar. Then write the days of the week and the dates of the month on the calendar.
3. Write holidays, birthdays, and other important dates on your calendar.
4. Decorate your calendar.
5. Present your calendar to the class. Hang it on the wall.

November

Sunday	Monday	Tuesday	Wednesday	Thursday	Friday	Saturday
	1	2	3	4	5	6
7	8	9	10	11	12	13
14	15	16	17	18	19	20
21	22	23	24	25 Thanksgiving	26 Vacation	27
28	29 School Concert	30				

CHAPTER 2

About My Family

Objectives

Listening and Speaking describing people

Grammar present tense of *be*

Word Study long vowels: *a, i, o, u*

Reading poem

Writing description of a family member

Content Activity Book: science

dog

cat

bird

fish

father

grandmother

brother

mother

sister

grandfather

Listen, Speak, Interact

That's My Mother

Words to Know

beautiful

handsome

cute

1 🎧 **Listen and repeat.** Listen and repeat the words.

2 🎧 **Listen and repeat.** Listen to the conversation. Then repeat the conversation.

Student A:	Who's that?
Student B:	That's my mother.
Student A:	Your mother is beautiful.
Student B:	Thanks.

3 **Pair work.** Practice the conversation with a partner.

Student A:	Who's that?
Student B:	That's my ____ .
Student A:	Your ____ is ____ .
Student B:	Thanks.

4 **Pair work.** Draw a picture of a person in your family. Talk about the person with your partner.

Build Vocabulary

Adjectives

Adjectives describe people, places, or things.

5 🎧 **Listen and repeat.** Look at the pictures. Listen to the adjectives. Repeat the adjectives.

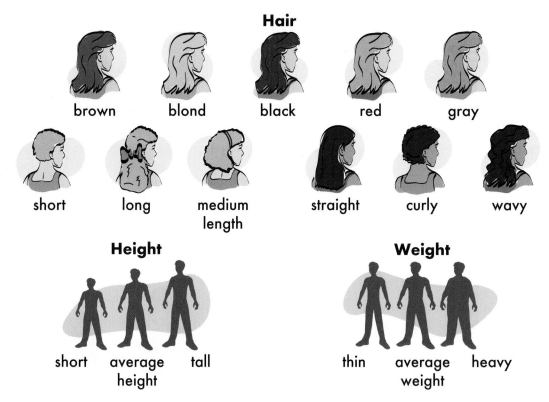

Hair

brown   blond   black   red   gray

short   long   medium length   straight   curly   wavy

Height

short   average height   tall

Weight

thin   average weight   heavy

6 **Write.** Think of a famous person. What adjectives describe the person? Write the adjectives on a piece of paper.

7 **Pair work.** Think of someone you know. What adjectives describe the person? Tell your partner. Your partner will draw the person.

Activity Book
Page 41

Grammar Focus

Simple Present of *be*

Use the **simple present of *be*** to give information.

Simple Present: *be*		
I	**am**	a student.
You	**are**	tall.
He	**is**	my brother.
She	**is**	17.
It	**is**	heavy.
We	**are**	friends.
They	**are**	sisters.

8 **Build the sentence.** Add the right form of *be*.

1. She __is__ a student.

2. I ___ from Mexico.

3. They ___ not teachers.

4. His eyes ___ not blue.

5. We ___ friends.

6. The dog ___ cute.

9 **Choose.** Which sentence is true about you?

1. I am a student.
   I am not a student.

2. I am tall.
   I am not tall.

3. My hair is brown.
   My hair is not brown.

Negative
I am **not** thin.
You are **not** tall.

Contractions
I am = I'm
you are = you're
he is = he's
she is = she's
it is = it's
we are = we're
they are = they're

10 **Write.** Write three true sentences about yourself.

I'm from Russia.
I'm 16.
My eyes are brown.

Activity Book
Pages 42–43

Word Study

Long Vowels: a, i, o, u

Long vowels make the sound of their name.

Long Vowels	
Long a:	face, cake, make, date
Long i:	like, kite, nice, white
Long o:	nose, note, phone, stove
Long u:	cute, June, rule, tube

11 🎧 **Listen and repeat.** Listen to the long vowel. Then listen to the long vowel in each word. Repeat each word.

12 🎧 **Listen.** Listen to the words. Which word has a long vowel sound? Can you find a pattern?

1. can   cane
2. kite   kit
3. hope   hop
4. cut   cute
5. mad   made

> Pronunciation Pattern
> Do you see the letter **e** at the end of a word? Then pronounce the first vowel in the word with a long vowel sound.

13 **Pair work.** With a partner, say these words.

1. can   4. rob
2. tub   5. mad
3. spin   6. car

Now add the letter *e* to the end of the words. Say the new words.

Activity Book
Page 44

Into the Reading

────────

You will read a poem. In this poem, a sister describes her new baby brother.

Use Prior Knowledge: Describe a Baby

What adjectives describe a baby? Brainstorm a list with a partner.

	Baby
1.	small
2.	loud
3.	
4.	
5.	

Build Background: Dimples

Many babies have dimples. A dimple is a small dent in the skin.

dimple

Reading and Understanding

Text Structure: Poem

A **poem** sometimes has:
- adjectives
- words that rhyme

Look and listen for adjectives and words that rhyme in the poem.

Words that **rhyme** sound almost the same.

   cat   hat

Only the sound of the first part of the word is different.

🎧 Reading

My Baby Brother
a poem by Mary Ann Hoberman

My baby brother's beautiful,
So perfect and so tiny.
His skin is soft and velvet brown;
His eyes are dark and shiny.

His hair is black and curled up tight;
His two new teeth are sharp and white.
I like it when he chews his toes;
And when he laughs, his dimple shows.

Beyond the Reading

Reading comprehension. Answer the questions.

1. Is the baby large?
2. Is his hair brown or black?
3. How many teeth does he have?
4. What adjectives in the poem describe the baby?

Find words that rhyme. Look at the last word in each line of the poem.

1. Find the words that rhyme.
2. Find the vowel sound in the words that rhyme. Are they short vowel sounds or long vowel sounds?

Shared reading. With a partner, listen again to the audio recording of the poem. Practice reading the poem. You read one line. Your partner reads the next line.

Activity Book
Pages 45–46

From Reading to Writing

Describing a Family Member

Draw a picture of a person in your family.
Then write a description of the person.

My Grandmother

My grandmother is short.
Her hair is black and curly.
She is very kind.
My grandmother is beautiful.

Jin Kong

Step 1. Plan

a. Choose a person to write about. Think about the person.
   Is the person short or tall? Is the person heavy or thin?
b. Draw a picture of the person.

Step 2. Write

Write four sentences about the person. Who is the person?
What does the person look like? Use adjectives in your
sentences. Use adjectives you know. Use a dictionary to
find new adjectives.

VISIONS

Activity Book
Page 47

Step 3. Edit

a. Read your sentences. Can you find any mistakes?
b. Check your sentences with the Editing Checklist.

Step 4. Publish

a. Correct any mistakes in your sentences.
b. Write the sentences again. You may want to write the sentences on a computer.
c. Read your sentences to the class.
d. Display your work in class.

VISIONS

Activity Book
Page 48

Review

Student
CD-ROM

VOCABULARY I can read and spell these words.

Family members

mother	sister	grandmother
father	brother	grandfather

Pets

bird	cat	dog	fish

Adjectives

average height	beautiful	handsome	medium length	tall
average weight	blond	heavy	short	thin
	curly	height	straight	wavy
	gray	long		weight

Expressions

Who's that?   That's my .

GRAMMAR I can use this grammar.
Simple Present of *be*

I	**am**	tall.
You / We / They	**are**	tall.
He / She / It	**is**	tall.

WORD STUDY I can pronounce these long vowels.
Long Vowels

long a: face   **long i:** bike   **long o:** nose   **long u:** tube

Assess

VOCABULARY

1. My father is ____ .

    a. handsome   **b.** height   **c.** wavy   **d.** blue

Review pages 66-68.

2. My baby ____ is cute.

    a. mother   **b.** grandfather   **c.** sister   **d.** father

3. His eyes are ____ .

    a. heavy   **b.** wavy   **c.** blond   **d.** blue

GRAMMAR

1. I ____ 15 years old.

    a. is   **b.** are   **c.** am

Review page 69.

2. The dog ____ brown.

    a. are   **b.** am   **c.** is

3. We ____ friends.

    a. am   **b.** is   **c.** are

WORD STUDY   What is the vowel sound?

Review page 70.

1.

    a. long o
    b. long a
    c. long i
    d. long u

2.

    a. long a
    b. long o
    c. long i
    d. long u

Projects

Project 1: Family Member Presentation

Give a presentation about a family member, a pet,
or someone else important to you.

1. Choose a person to tell the class about. Find a photograph
   or draw a picture of this person.

2. Write notes about this person for your presentation.
   Include adjectives in your notes. Practice your presentation.

3. Give your presentation. Use your notes. Show your
   photograph or drawing. Make sure you:

   a. speak slowly

   b. speak clearly

   c. make eye contact with
      your classmates

4. Evaluate your presentation
   with this checklist.

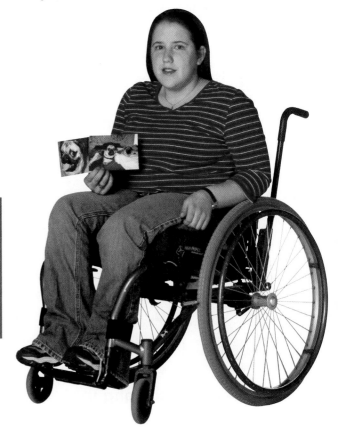

Presentation Checklist
☐ I spoke slowly.
☐ I spoke clearly.
☐ I made eye contact.

Project 2: Make and Organize Rhyme Cards

Work with a small group to make and organize rhyme cards.

1. Copy these words onto note cards. Put one word on each card.

lip	date	late	hip
hat	gate	kite	tight
cat	make	rip	drip
white	bake	take	mat
sat	bat	plate	right

2. Which words rhyme? With your group, organize the cards into groups of words that rhyme.

3. Try to add more words to each group of words that rhyme.

4. Read each set of words that rhyme to your class.

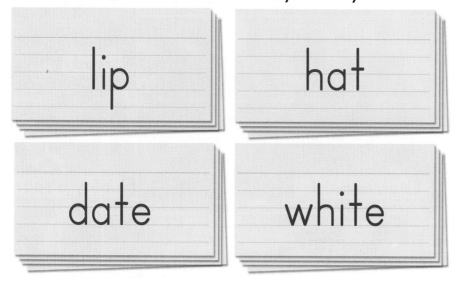

Objectives

Listening and Speaking talking about activities

Grammar simple present

Word Study long *e* sound: *ee, ea*

Reading free verse poem

Writing paragraph about a favorite activity

Content Activity Book: the arts

work

play an instrument

meet friends

read

write e-mail

listen to music

play a sport

shop

rent a video

Listen, Speak, Interact

What Do You Do After School?

1 🎧 **Listen and repeat.** Listen and repeat the words and phrases.

2 🎧 **Listen and repeat.** Listen to the conversation. Repeat the conversation.

A: What do you usually do after school?

B: I usually work after school.

A: What else do you do?

B: I sometimes meet friends.

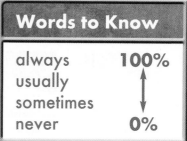

Words to Know	
always	**100%**
usually	
sometimes	
never	**0%**

3 **Pair work.** Practice the conversation with a partner. Complete the sentences with information about you.

A: What do you usually do after school?

B: I usually _____ after school.

A: What else do you do?

B: I sometimes _____ .

4 **Pair work.** What do you *always* do after class? What do you *usually* do? What do you *sometimes* do? What do you *never* do? Tell your partner.

Build Vocabulary

Activities

5 🎧 **Listen and repeat.** Look at the pictures. Listen to the words. Repeat the words.

Sports

exercise   jog   swim   play soccer   play baseball

Arts

paint   write   dance   play the guitar   play the drums

6 **Pair work.** Talk about the activities. How often do you do each activity? Often? Sometimes? Never?

7 **Organize.** Which activity is each object for? Copy the chart. Put the words in the correct columns.

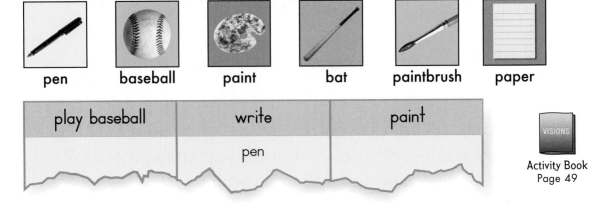

pen   baseball   paint   bat   paintbrush   paper

play baseball	write	paint
	pen	

VISIONS

Activity Book
Page 49

Grammar Focus

Simple Present

Simple Present	
I	read.
You	read.
He	reads.
She	reads.
It	reads.
We	read.
They	read.

Use the **simple present** to tell about an action that usually happens or is happening now.

8 **Build the sentence.** Choose a verb from the box. Add an **s** to the verb if necessary.

read	play	meet	work	eat

1. I always <u>play</u> soccer on Saturday.

2. My mother ____ the newspaper in the morning.

3. We sometimes ____ our friends after school.

4. The dog ____ all of its food.

5. The secretary ____ in the school office.

> Verbs are action words. Read, swim, play, and work are verbs.

9 **Choose.** Which sentence is true about you?

1. I work after school.
I do not work after school.

2. I play an instrument.
I do not play an instrument.

3. I exercise every day.
I do not exercise every day.

> Negative
> I/You/We/They do not read.
> He/She/It does not read.

Activity Book
Pages 50–51

Word Study

Long e sound: ee, ea

Long e sound	
ee: feet, green, meet, teeth, street	
ea: eat, ear, teach, team, seat	

These vowels together make the sound of the letter *e:* **ee, ea.**

10 🎧 **Listen and repeat.** Listen to the long *e* sound. Then listen to the long *e* sound in each word. Repeat each word.

11 **Read and find.** Find the words in the poem with the long *e* sound.

> After school, who do I meet?
> I meet my friends down the street.
> What do we do down the street?
> We talk, we shop, and we always eat!

12 **Pair work.** Take turns reading the poem with a partner.

13 **Read.** Say the words.

1. cheek   4. greet
2. meal   5. east
3. speech   6. real

Activity Book
Page 52

Into the Reading

You will read a poem. The poem is about a girl. The girl tries a new activity for the first time.

Use Prior Knowledge: Trying Something New

You are trying to learn a new activity. How do you feel? Copy the word web on a piece of paper. Fill it in with a partner.

Strategy

Preview Pictures
Before you read, look at the picture. A picture can give you information about the reading. This information helps you understand the reading.

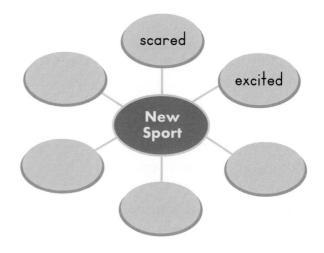

Build Background: Roller Skating

Roller skating is a kind of sport. You wear special shoes called roller skates. Roller skates have wheels on the bottom. Roller skating is difficult at first. You must practice this activity.

Reading and Understanding

Text Structure: Free Verse Poem

In Chapter 2 you read a poem with words that rhyme. Some poems do not have words that rhyme. These poems are **free verse poems.**

🎧 Reading

74th Street

a poem by Myra Cohn Livingston

Hey, this little kid gets roller skates.
She puts them on.
She stands up and almost
hops over backwards.
She sticks out a foot like
she's going somewhere and
falls down and
smacks her hand. She
grabs hold of a step to get up and
sticks out the other foot and
slides about six inches and
falls and
skins her knee.

        And then, you know what?

She brushes off the dirt and the
blood and puts some
spit on it and then
sticks out the other foot

    again.

Beyond the Reading

Reading comprehension. Answer the questions.

1. Does the girl hurt her knee or her foot?
2. How many times does she fall?
3. What does she grab?
4. What does the girl do after she falls?

Organize pictures. Look at the pictures. Put them in order.

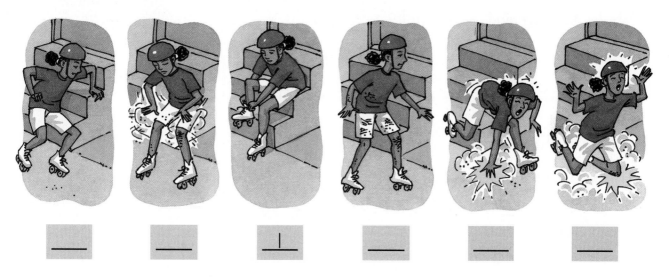

___	___	_1_	___	___	___

Retell the story. Work with a partner. Use the pictures to tell the events in the poem. Tell the events in the right order.

Act out the poem. Work with a partner. One partner reads the poem. The other partner does the actions in the poem.

Activity Book
Pages 53–54

From Reading to Writing

My Favorite Activity

Write a paragraph about your favorite activity.

> ### Soccer
>
> Soccer is my favorite sport. I play soccer every weekend. Soccer is fun. You do not need a lot of equipment. You need a soccer ball, some friends, and a place to play.
>
> Diego Torrez

Paragraph
A paragraph is a group of sentences. The sentences are about the same subject. Indent the first line of a paragraph.

Step 1. Plan

Think about these questions:
a. What is your favorite activity?
b. When do you do it?
c. Do you need any special objects or equipment?

Step 2. Write

Write a paragraph about your favorite activity.
Write three or four sentences. Give your paragraph a title.

Activity Book
Page 55

Step 3. Edit

a. Read your paragraph. Can you find any mistakes?
b. Check the sentences in your paragraph. Use the Editing Checklist.

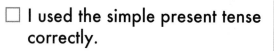

☐ The sentences begin with a capital letter.

☐ The sentences end with a period.

☐ The sentences are in a paragraph.

☐ I indented the first line of the paragraph.

☐ I used the simple present tense correctly.

Step 4. Publish

a. Correct any mistakes in your paragraph.
b. Write the paragraph again. You may want to write the paragraph on a computer.
c. Read your paragraph to the class.
d. Hang up your paragraph in the classroom.

Activity Book
Page 56

Review

Student
CD-ROM

VOCABULARY I can read and spell these words.

Activities

dance	play a sport	rent a video
exercise	play baseball	roller skate
jog	play soccer	shop
listen to music	play the drums	swim
meet friends	play the guitar	work
paint	read	write e-mail
play an instrument		

Objects

baseball	drums	paint	paper
bat	guitar	paintbrush	roller skates

Frequency words

always	usually	sometimes	never

GRAMMAR I can use this grammar.

Simple Present

I / You / We / They	**read.**
He / She / It	**reads.**

WORD STUDY I can pronounce this long vowel sound.

Long e sound: ee, ea

ee: **teeth**   ea: **eat**

Assess

VOCABULARY

1. I ____ soccer every Saturday.

    a. eat   **b.** dance   **c.** play   **d.** listen

2. He always ____ the newspaper.

    a. reads   **b.** listens   **c.** rents   **d.** speaks

3. I want to play baseball. I need a baseball and a ____ .

    a. pen   **b.** bat   **c.** paintbrush   **d.** soccer ball

Review pages 80-82.

GRAMMAR

1. We ____ at the gym.

    a. exercise   **b.** exercises

2. My mother ____ beautiful pictures.

    a. paint   **b.** paints

3. ____ listens to music.

    a. She   **b.** We   **c.** They

Review page 83.

WORD STUDY   Say the words.

1. feel   **3.** eat   **5.** seat

2. need   **4.** speech   **6.** teach

Review page 84.

Projects

Project 1: Activities Collage

Work with a small group to make a poster of your favorite activities.

1. Discuss your favorite activities with your group.
2. Make a list of your group's favorite activities.
3. Find and cut out pictures of the activities. Use old magazines or newspapers. You can also draw pictures of the activities.
4. Paste your pictures on poster board. Label the activities.
5. Hang up the poster in your classroom.

Project 2: Favorite Activity Presentation

Give a presentation about your favorite activity.

1. What is your favorite activity? Find a photograph or draw a picture of the activity.
2. What equipment do you need? Find the words in a bilingual dictionary. If possible, bring in the equipment for your presentation.
3. Write notes for your presentation. Write notes about:
   a. your favorite activity
   b. the equipment you need for the activity
   c. when you do the activity
4. Practice your presentation.
5. Give your presentation. Use your notes.
   Show your photograph or drawing.
   Show the equipment. Make sure you:
   a. speak slowly
   b. speak clearly
   c. make eye contact with your classmates
6. Evaluate your presentation with this checklist.

Presentation Checklist
☐ I spoke slowly.
☐ I spoke clearly.
☐ I made eye contact.

CHAPTER 4   Home

Objectives

Listening and Speaking talking about activities in different rooms

Grammar *there is / there are*

Word Study compound words

Reading vignette

Writing paragraph about a future home

Content Activity Book: social studies

apartment

kitchen

living room

apartment building

bedroom

bathroom

house

Listen, Speak, Interact

I Study in the Living Room

1 🎧 **Listen and repeat.** Listen and repeat the words.

2 🎧 **Listen and repeat.** Listen to the conversation.
Then repeat the conversation.

A: What do you do in the living room?
B: I watch TV in the living room.
A: What else do you do in the living room?
B: I study in the living room.

3 **Pair work.** Practice the conversation.
Complete the sentences with
information about you.

A: What do you do in the ___ ?

B: I ___ in the ___ .

A: What else do you do in the ___ ?

B: I ___ in the bathroom.

4 **Group work.** What activities do you
do in the kitchen? Brainstorm a list with
your group. Ask your teacher for help
or use a bilingual dictionary.

In the Bathroom

take a
shower

brush
my teeth

In the Bedroom

sleep

read

In the Kitchen

cook

eat

Build Vocabulary

What's in the Room?

5 🎧 **Listen and repeat.** Look at the pictures. Listen to the words. Repeat the words.

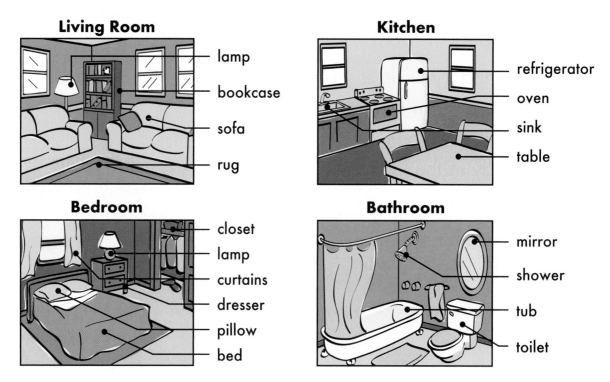

Living Room

- lamp
- bookcase
- sofa
- rug

Kitchen

- refrigerator
- oven
- sink
- table

Bedroom

- closet
- lamp
- curtains
- dresser
- pillow
- bed

Bathroom

- mirror
- shower
- tub
- toilet

6 **Find the word.** Unscramble the letters to find the word. Match the word to the picture.

a. **b.** **c.** **d.**

Activity Book
Page 57

1. <u>a</u> deb   **2.** __ aofs   **3.** __ nksi   **4.** __ erfrigtrearo

Grammar Focus

There Is / There Are

Use *there is* to talk about one noun. Use *there are* to talk about more than one.

> **There is** a chair in the room.
>
> **There is** a window in the room.
>
> **There are** (two) chairs in the room.
>
> **There are** (four) windows in the room.

7 **Build sentences.** Look at the pictures on page 96. Make true sentences with phrases from each column below.

Example: There is an oven in the kitchen.

	an oven	in the bathroom.
There is	two pillows	in the living room.
There are	two sofas	in the bedroom.
	a shower	in the kitchen.

> A phrase is a part of a sentence.

> Plural s
> To make most nouns plural, add an s:
> chair / chairs
> window / windows

8 **Pair work.** Look at the pictures on page 96. Talk about each room with your partner. Use *there is / there are.*

Activity Book
Pages 58–59

Word Study
Compound Words

Strategy

Word Recognition
Look at the two smaller words in a compound word. This can help you understand the compound word.

A **compound word** is a word made from two smaller words.

9 Read and find. Find the smaller words in these compound words.

1. classroom class room

2. backpack ____ ____

3. bathtub ____ ____

4. bedroom ____ ____

5. football ____ ____

6. notebook ____ ____

10 🎧 Listen. Listen to the smaller words in the compound word. Then listen to the compound word.

11 Read and understand. These are new compound words. Look for the smaller words to understand the compound word. Then match the compound words to the pictures.

1. _f_ armchair

2. __ birdhouse

3. __ mailbox

4. __ waterfall

5. __ hairbrush

6. __ headphones

a.

b.

c.

d.

e.

f.

Activity Book
Page 60

Into the Reading

Strategy

Predict
Before you read, look at the title of the reading. Look at the pictures. Predict what the reading will be about.

You will read a writer's thoughts about her home.

Use Prior Knowledge: Feelings About Home

Think of your home. What do you see? What do you hear? What do you feel? What do you taste? What do you smell? Look at the model. Then copy the chart. Fill in the chart with your own ideas.

see	hear	feel	taste	smell
family photos	the TV	soft couch	fresh bread	food

Build Background: Petunias

Petunias are large flowers. They grow outside and need a lot of sun. Petunias grow in large groups. They are usually purple, pink, or white.

Reading and Understanding

Text Structure: Vignette

A vignette is a short, descriptive reading. It usually has a theme or main subject. It tells how the writer feels about the subject. The theme of this vignette is "home." As you read, think about this question: How does the author feel about her home?

flat = apartment

Reading

A House of My Own
a vignette by Sandra Cisneros

Not a flat. Not an apartment in back. Not a man's house. Not a daddy's. A house all my own. With my porch and my pillows, my pretty purple petunias. My books and my stories. My two shoes waiting beside the bed. Nobody to shake a stick at. Nobody's garbage to pick up after.

Only a house quiet as snow, a space for myself to go, clean as paper before the poem.

Beyond the Reading

Reading comprehension. Answer the questions.

1. Does the author have a home of her own?
2. Does she have an apartment or a house?
3. What does she have in her home?
4. What adjectives in the poem describe her home?

Think about the picture. Look at the picture next to the reading. What do you see in the picture? What did you predict? Were you right?

Compare with words. The writer uses the word *as* to compare her house and other things:

> Only a house *quiet as snow*, a space for myself to go, *clean as paper* before the poem.

Can you think of other things to compare her house to?

The house is quiet as ____ .

The house is clean as ____ .

Activity Book
Page 61–62

From Reading to Writing

My Future Home

Imagine your future home. Write a paragraph about it.

My Future Home

My future home is a large house. I live in the house with my husband and two children. There are six rooms in the house. There are three bedrooms, a bathroom, a kitchen, and a living room. There is also a garden and a porch. There is a comfortable couch and a big TV in the living room.

Alicia Morales

Step 1. Plan

Think about your future home. Is it a house or an apartment? How many rooms are there? What objects are there? What people are there? Copy this cluster map on a piece of paper. Fill it out.

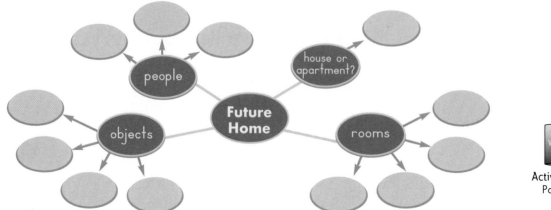

VISIONS

Activity Book
Page 63

Step 2. Write

a. Write a paragraph about your future home.
Use the ideas from your cluster map.
b. Use *there is / there are* to talk about the rooms,
objects, and people in your home.
c. Give your paragraph a title.

Step 3. Edit

Read your paragraph. Can
you find any mistakes? Use the
Editing Checklist.

Step 4. Publish

a. Correct any mistakes in your
paragraph.
b. Write the paragraph again.
You may want to type the
paragraph on a computer.

Editing Checklist

☐ The sentences begin with
a capital letter.

☐ The sentences end with
a period.

☐ The sentences are in
a paragraph.

☐ I indented the first line of the
paragraph.

☐ I used *there is / there are*
correctly.

c. Draw a picture of one of the rooms in your home.
Make sure the drawing matches the description of the house in
the paragraph.
d. Read your paragraph to the class. Show your picture.
e. Post your paragraph in the classroom.

VISIONS

Activity Book
Page 64

Review

VOCABULARY I can read and spell these words.

apartment   apartment building   house

In the home

bathroom	curtain	oven	shower
bathtub	dresser	pillow	sink
bed	kitchen	radio	sofa
bedroom	lamp	refrigerator	table
bookcase	living room	rug	toilet
closet	mirror		

GRAMMAR I can use this grammar.
there is / there are

There is a chair.   **There are** chairs.

There is a window.   **There are** windows.

WORD STUDY I can understand compound words.
Compound Words

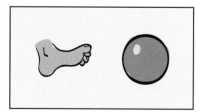

foot + ball = football   bird + house = birdhouse   note + book = notebook

Assess

VOCABULARY

Review pages 94–96.

1. I cook in the ____ .

    a. bathroom   **b.** living room   **c.** kitchen   **d.** bedroom

2. The ____ is on the bed.

    a. bookcase   **b.** couch   **c.** pillow   **d.** stove

3. The ____ is in the bathroom.

    a. couch   **b.** refrigerator   **c.** bed   **d.** toilet

GRAMMAR

Review page 97.

1. There ____ five rooms in my home.

    a. is   **b.** are

2. There ____ a pillow on the bed.

    a. is   **b.** are

3. There are two ____ in the kitchen.

    a. window   **b.** windows

WORD STUDY Match the words and pictures.

Review page 98.

1. __ haircut   **2.** __ handbag   **3.** __ earring

a.

b.

c.

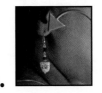

Projects

Project 1: Create Your Dream Home

Make a floor plan of your dream home.

1. Discuss your dream home with a partner.
2. Make a list of the rooms and objects in your dream home.
3. Draw the floor plan of your home on a piece of poster paper.
4. Find and cut out pictures of the objects for each room. Use old magazines, newspapers, or catalogs. You can also draw pictures of the objects.
5. Paste the objects in the right rooms. Label the objects.
6. Hang up the poster in your classroom.

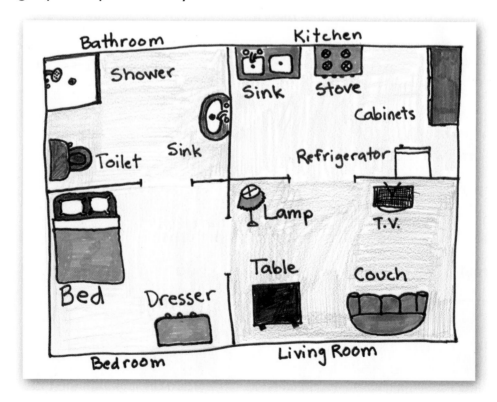

Project 2: Find Compound Nouns

Work with a small group to create word cards. Create compound nouns with the cards.

1. Copy these words onto index cards. Put one word on each card.

pack	class	foot	note
birth	bath	brush	board
paint	ball	mate	back
book	day	room	black

2. With your group, match the cards to find compound words.

3. Draw a picture for each compound word you find.

4. Show the class the compound words and pictures.

CHAPTER 5

The Community

Objectives

Listening and Speaking talking about community places, transportation, and time

Grammar present continuous

Word Study digraphs: *ch, sh, th, wh, ng*

Reading newspaper articles

Writing informational paragraph

Content Activity Book: social studies

video store

post office

supermarket

park

movie theater

hospital

library

bus

train

walk

car

Listen, Speak, Interact

How Do You Get There?

1 Listen and repeat. Listen and repeat the words.

2 Listen and repeat. Listen to the conversation. Then repeat the conversation.

A: How do you get to the library?

B: I take the bus. How about you?

A: I walk.

3 Pair work. Look at the community places on page 108. Ask your partner how he or she gets to each place.

A: How do you get to the ___ ?

B: I ___ . How about you?

A: I ___ .

Build Vocabulary

Time

4 🎧 **Listen and repeat.** Look at the clocks. Listen and repeat the times.

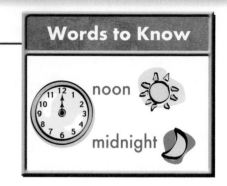

Words to Know

noon

midnight

1:00	1:05	1:15	1:30	1:45	1:55

| one o'clock | one oh five | one fifteen | one thirty | one forty-five | one fifty-five |

5 **Pair work.** Look at the classroom clock or a watch. What time is it now? Tell your partner. Write the time.

Words to Know

AM = morning, day
PM = afternoon, evening

6 **Read and answer.** Read the bus schedule. Answer the questions.

1. It's 7:00 AM. What time is the next bus?

The next bus is at 7:15 AM.

2. It's 8:45 AM.
What time is the next bus?

3. It's 10:30 AM.
What time is the next bus?

4. It's 5:10 PM.
What time is the next bus?

5. It's 6:30 PM.
What time is the next bus?

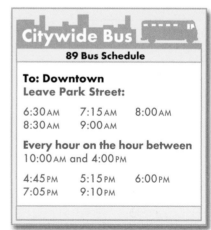

Citywide Bus

89 Bus Schedule

To: Downtown
Leave Park Street:

6:30 AM   7:15 AM   8:00 AM
8:30 AM   9:00 AM

Every hour on the hour between
10:00 AM and 4:00 PM

4:45 PM   5:15 PM   6:00 PM
7:05 PM   9:10 PM

VISIONS

Activity Book
Page 65

Grammar Focus

Present Continuous

The **present continuous** tells about an action happening right now.

Present Continuous		
I	am	reading.
You	are	reading.
He	is	reading.
She	is	reading.
It	is	reading.
We	are	reading.
They	are	reading.

-ing Spelling Rules

Add -*ing* to the end of most verbs:

    walk ⟶ *walking*

For verbs that end in e, drop the e and add -*ing*:

    dance ⟶ *dancing*

For verbs with one syllable that end in a vowel and a consonant, double the consonant and add -*ing*:

    run ⟶ *running*

7 **Read and find.** Read the poem. Find the present continuous sentences. Then find the present tense sentences. How are they different?

8 **Write.** Look around your class. What are people doing? Write present continuous sentences.

A Circle of Sun
by Rebecca Kai Dotlich

I'm dancing.
I'm leaping.
I'm skipping about.
I gallop.
I grin.
I giggle.
I shout.
I'm Earth's many colors.
I'm morning and night.
I'm honey on toast.
I'm funny.
I'm bright.
I'm swinging.
I'm singing.
I wiggle.
I run.
I'm a piece of the sky
In a circle of sun.

Activity Book
Pages 66–67

Word Study

Digraphs: *ch, sh, th, wh, ng*

These two consonants
together make one sound:
ch, sh, th, wh, ng.

Digraphs	
ch:	cheek, child, chin, porch
sh:	she, shop, fish, bookshelf
th:	bath, thank, three, teeth
wh:	white, when, where, why
ng:	wing, finger, sing, reading

9 🎧 **Listen and repeat.** Listen to the
sound the two consonants make together.
Then listen to the sound in each word.
Repeat each word.

> All verbs in the
> present continuous
> have the **ng** sound
> at the end.

10 **Write.** What are the missing letters?
Choose: *ch, sh, th, wh,* or *ng.*

  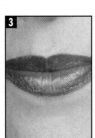  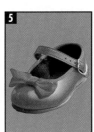 

1. <u>sh</u> irt   2. ___ air   3. mou ___   4. ___ eel   5. ___ oe   6. ri ___

11 🎧 **Listen and choose.** Look at the pair of words. Listen.
Which word do you hear?

1. thin   chin   4. when   then
2. math   mat   5. choose   shoes
3. sink   think   6. hop   shop

VISIONS

Activity Book
Page 68

Into the Reading

You will read three short
articles. The articles are from
a community newspaper.

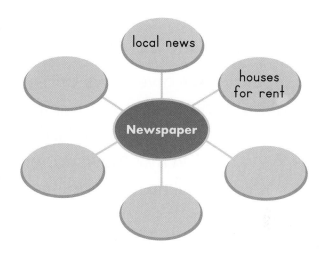

Use Prior Knowledge: Newspapers

What information can you
find in a newspaper?

Build Background: Community Service

Community service is work you do for free in your community.
Community service helps people and places in your community.

Reading and Understanding

Text Structure: Newspaper Article

Newspaper articles give news and information about events happening now. They answer questions like: *Who? What? When? Where? Why?* Newspaper articles begin with a headline. A headline is a short title.

Reading

The Brookdale Community News

Brookdale Soccer Team Always Scores a Goal

Brookdale loves its soccer team. The Brookdale Bears always play an exciting game. There is a game at Clark Park every Saturday afternoon at 1:00. Tickets are free for students, senior citizens, and children under 12.

Brookdale Mall Opens

A new mall is opening in Brookdale today! The Brookdale Downtown Mall is on 300 Main Street, next to the library. The mall is open every day from 9:00AM to 7:00PM. Hurry to the mall today. The manager is giving away free T-shirts to the first 100 customers.

Students Help Elderly

Some students from Brookdale High School are doing community service work at the Washington Home for the Elderly today. These students are helping the residents in many ways. Some students are reading to the residents. Some are helping the residents shop. Some are bringing residents to doctor appointments. The students are showing the community that kids care!

Beyond the Reading

Reading comprehension. Answer the questions.

1. Are Brookdale students helping the elderly?
2. Do the Brookdale Bears play soccer on Saturday or Sunday?
3. What is the manager of the Brookdale Mall giving away today?
4. Which article is most interesting to you? Why?

Scan for information. Copy the chart. Look at the questions.
Scan the reading for the information. Fill out the chart.

	Students Help Elderly	Brookdale Soccer Team Always Scores a Goal	Brookdale Mall Opens
Who is the article about?	students residents		
What is the article about?	community work		
When is the event happening?	today		
Where is the event happening?	the Washington Home for the Elderly		

Activity Book
Pages 69–70

From Reading to Writing

Informational Paragraph

An informational paragraph gives information. It answers questions like *who, what, when, where,* and *why.* Write an informational paragraph about something in your school or community.

Dance Class

Saturday is my favorite day. On Saturday I take dance class. I study Latin dance at the Pittsfield Community Center on Green Street. The class is from 10:00 to 11:30 AM. I always have fun in my dance class.

Rosa Alvarez

Step 1. Plan

a. Choose a subject for your paragraph. You may write about a class, a sports team, an event, or a shop in your community.

b. Think about the subject of your paragraph. What do you know about the subject? Copy the sunshine organizer and fill it out with this information.

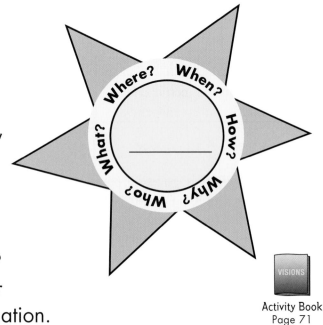

Activity Book
Page 71

Step 2. Write

Write a paragraph about your subject. Use the first sentence to tell what the paragraph is about. Then give more information about your subject in the next sentences. Use the information from your sunshine organizer.

Step 3. Edit

Read your paragraph. Can you find any mistakes? Check your paragraph. Use the Editing Checklist.

Step 4. Publish

a. Correct any problems in your paragraph. Use the Editing Checklist to help you.

b. Copy the paragraph in your best handwriting. You may want to write the paragraph on a computer.

c. Read your paragraph to the class. Hang up your paragraph in the classroom.

Editing Checklist
☐ The sentences are in a paragraph.
☐ I indented the first line of the paragraph.
☐ I wrote about a subject.
☐ I included information about the subject.

Activity Book
Page 72

Review

VOCABULARY I can read and spell these words.

Community places

community center	library	park	restaurant
fire station	mall	police station	supermarket
hospital	movie theater	post office	video store

Transportation

car / drive   train / take the train   bus / take the bus   walk
ride a bike

Time

AM	1:00 = one o'clock	1:45 = one forty-five
PM	1:05 = one oh five	1:55 = one fifty-five
noon	1:15 = one fifteen	
midnight	1:30 = one thirty	

Question words

who   what   where   when   why

Expressions

How do you get to ____ ?   What time is it?

GRAMMAR I can use this grammar.

Present Continuous

I	**am**	read**ing.**
You / We / They	**are**	read**ing.**
He / She / It	**is**	read**ing.**

WORD STUDY I can pronounce these digraphs.

Digraphs: *ch, sh, th, wh, ng*

ch: **ch**ild   sh: **fish**   th: **three**   wh: **wh**en   ng: ri**ng**

Assess

VOCABULARY

Review pages 108-110.

1. My mother buys food at the ____ .

   a. post office   **b.** park   **c.** supermarket   **d.** hospital

2. I get books at the ____ .

   a. supermarket   **b.** police station   **c.** park   **d.** library

3. ____ is the next bus?

   a. When   **b.** Why   **c.** How   **d.** Who

GRAMMAR

Review page 111.

1. My teacher ____ the computer now.

   a. are using   **b.** use   **c.** using   **d.** is using

2. I ____ the bus today.

   a. are taking   **b.** am taking   **c.** takes   **d.** am take

3. We are ____ the book.

   a. read   **b.** reads   **c.** reading   **d.** are reading

WORD STUDY Say these nonsense words.

Review page 112.

1. chim   **4.** lang

2. wheg   **5.** thrib

3. shob

Projects

Project 1: Make a Transportation Graph

Work with your class. How do the students in your class get to school? Create a bar graph.

1. Ask: *Who takes the train to school?* Count how many students take the train to school. Record the number.
2. Ask: *Who takes the bus to school?* Count how many students take the bus to school. Record the number.
3. Ask: *Who drives to school?* Count how many students drive to school. Record the number.
4. Ask: *Who walks to school?* Count how many students walk to school. Record the number.
5. Ask: *Who rides a bike to school?* Count how many students ride a bike to school. Record the number.
6. Draw an empty bar graph on a large piece of poster paper.
7. Fill in each column on the graph.
8. Talk about the graph. How many students take each form of transportation?

8					
7					
6					
5					
4					
3					
2					
1					
	train	bus	car	walk	bike

Project 2: Create a School Newspaper

Work with your class to create a school newspaper.

1. Brainstorm subjects for news articles with your class. You may write about school events, sports teams, concerts, classes, and special programs.

2. Work in small groups. Each group writes one article.

   a. Write a headline for your article.

   b. Answer one or more of these questions in your article: *Who? What? When? Where? Why?*

   c. You may want to add a photograph or draw a picture.

3. Check your article for mistakes.

4. Type the article on a computer.

5. On a large piece of poster paper, write the name of your newspaper. Then paste the article to the paper. Include photographs or drawings.

6. Make copies of the newspaper. Give a copy to other classes.

Lincoln High School News

Lincoln High Prepares for January Concert

There is a lot of excitement at Lincoln High at the moment. Why? The school band is preparing for the January concert! The band is working hard to make sure this concert is a success. They are practicing every Tuesday and Thursday afternoon at 3:30. The concert is January 15. Tickets are available at the school office. They are free for students and their parents. Tickets are $5 for other community members.

CHAPTER 6 Food

Objectives

Listening and Speaking talking about food and diet

Grammar count and noncount nouns

Word Study plural count nouns

Reading informational text

Writing paragraph about diet

Content Activity Book: social studies

breakfast

toast

cereal

beef
bacon

eggs

lunch

soup

pizza

sandwich

hamburger

salad

dinner

peas

beans

rice

chicken

potatoes

steak

Listen, Speak, Interact

What Do You Eat for Breakfast?

1 🎧 **Listen and repeat.** Listen and repeat the words.

2 🎧 **Listen and repeat.** Listen to the conversation.
Then repeat the conversation.

A: What time do you eat breakfast?

B: I eat breakfast at 7:30.

A: What do you usually eat for breakfast?

B: I usually eat cereal for breakfast.

3 **Group work.** What foods do you eat for breakfast?
What do you eat for lunch? What do you eat for dinner?
Brainstorm a list of foods for each meal. Ask your teacher
for help or use a bilingual dictionary.

4 **Pair work.** Practice the conversation in Activity 2 again. This
time, complete the sentences with information about yourself.

Build Vocabulary

Setting the Table

How to Eat a Poem
by Eve Merriam

Don't be polite.
Bite in.
Pick it up with your fingers and lick the juice
        that may run down your chin.
It is ready and ripe now, whenever you are.
You do not need a knife or fork or spoon
or plate or napkin or tablecloth.
For there is no core
or stem
or rind
or pit
or seed
or skin
to throw away.

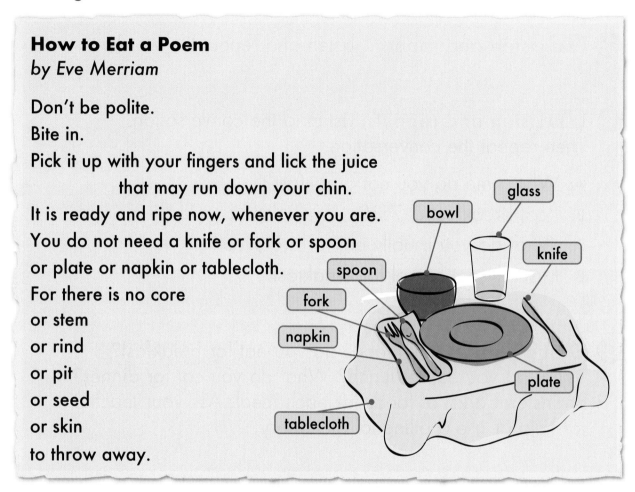

5 Listen and repeat. Listen and repeat the words.

6 Listen. Listen to the poem.

7 Pair work. Name a food. Your partner tells you what objects to use.

A: soup   B: bowl, spoon

Activity Book
Page 73

Grammar Focus

Count and Noncount Nouns

Count nouns are nouns that you can count.
Noncount nouns are:

   1. nouns that can't be counted (milk, rice)

   2. categories of things (money, furniture)

Count Nouns		
an orange / oranges	a hamburger / hamburgers	• have a singular form • have a plural form • can use numbers

Noncount Nouns		
juice	meat	• do not have a singular form • do not have a plural form • can't use numbers

8 Pair work. Can you count the food? Copy the chart.
Put each food in the correct column.

rice   hamburger   soup   potato   banana   fruit

Count	Noncount
hamburger	rice

Activity Book
Pages 74–75

Word Study

Plural Count Nouns: Spelling and Pronunciation

Plural Count Nouns: Spelling

Singular	Plural	Rule
fork egg	forks eggs	most nouns: add -s
sandwich potato	sandwiches potatoes	nouns that end in *ss, ch, sh, x,* or *consonant + vowel:* add -es
cherry family	cherries families	nouns that end in *consonant + y:* change *y* to *i* and add -es

9 Write. Write the plural form of each word.

    1. bowl   **3.** window   **5.** tomato   **7.** glass

    2. class   **4.** baby   **6.** city   **8.** chair

Plural Count Nouns: Pronunciation

There are three different ways to pronounce the -s or -es in plural nouns.

> **-s like in *books:*** cups, forks, steaks, tablecloths
> **-s like in *beds:*** eggs, beans, hamburgers, spoons
> **-es like in *classes:*** dishes, sandwiches, glasses

10 🎧 Listen and repeat. Listen to the different ways to pronounce the last sound in plural nouns. Repeat each word.

Activity Book
Page 76

Into the Reading

You will read a paragraph about food and diet.

Use Prior Knowledge: What Foods Are Healthy?

Talk to your partner. What foods are healthy? What foods are unhealthy? Copy the word webs onto a piece of paper. Fill them in with your partner.

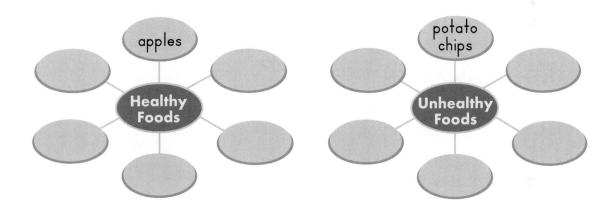

Build Background: Pyramids

A pyramid is a shape. Each side of a pyramid is a triangle. A triangle has three sides.

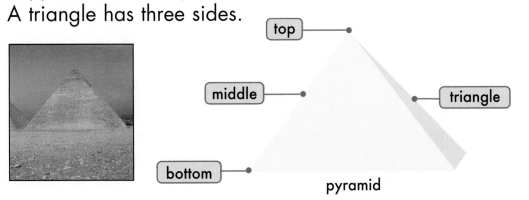

pyramid

Reading and Understanding

Text Structure: Informational Text

Informational texts explain and give information about a topic. As you read this text, think about these questions: What is the topic? What information does the text give about the topic?

> should = a good idea
> Use should before a verb.

🎧 Reading

The Food Guide Pyramid

The Food Guide Pyramid shows the six food groups. It tells how many servings you should eat from each group every day. Do you want to stay healthy? You should eat a lot of food from the bottom of the pyramid. The bread, cereal, rice, and pasta group is important for a healthy diet. You also need food from the middle of the pyramid. You should eat some food from the

Use sparingly
fats, oils, and sweets

2–3 servings
milk, yogurt, and cheese

3–5 servings
vegetable

2–3 servings
meat, poultry, fish, beans, eggs, and nuts

2–4 servings
fruit

6–11 servings
bread, cereal, rice, and pasta

vegetable and fruit groups every day. You also need a few servings from the milk, yogurt, and cheese group and the meat, poultry, fish, dry beans, eggs, and nuts group every day. You should eat very little food from the fats, oils, and sweets group at the top of the pyramid.

Beyond the Reading

Reading comprehension. Answer the questions.

1. Should you eat a lot of sweets?
2. Is bread at the top of the pyramid or the bottom of the pyramid?
3. How many servings of fruit should you eat each day?
4. What foods are very important for a healthy diet?

Analyze your diet. Make a list of all the foods you usually eat in a day. Put the foods into the food groups.

Compare your diet to the Food Guide Pyramid. Copy the chart. Fill in the number of servings of each food group you *should* eat. You can find this information in the reading. Fill in the number of servings you actually eat.

Food Group	Servings: I should eat...	Servings: I eat...
bread, cereal, rice, pasta	6-11	
vegetable		
fruit		
milk, yogurt, and cheese		
meat, poultry, fish, beans, eggs, and nuts		
fats, oils, and sweets		

Activity Book
Pages 77–78

From Reading to Writing

My Diet

Write a paragraph about your diet. Tell why your diet is healthy or why it is not healthy. Include a topic sentence and details.

> A topic sentence tells the main idea of a paragraph. The other sentences in the paragraph give details (information) about the main idea.

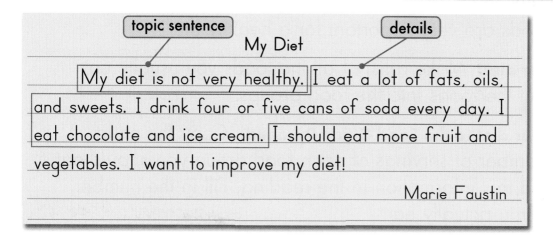

topic sentence · details

My Diet

My diet is not very healthy. I eat a lot of fats, oils, and sweets. I drink four or five cans of soda every day. I eat chocolate and ice cream. I should eat more fruit and vegetables. I want to improve my diet!

Marie Faustin

Step 1. Plan

a. Look at the Food Guide Pyramid on page 128. Compare your diet to the Food Guide Pyramid.

b. Talk to your partner about your diet. Do you have a healthy diet or an unhealthy diet? Tell your partner. Explain why your diet is healthy or why it is not healthy.

c. Write notes about your conversation. This will help you remember important details for your writing.

VISIONS

Activity Book
Page 79

Step 2. Write

Write a paragraph about your diet.

a. Begin your paragraph with a topic sentence.
b. Include details to support your topic sentence.
Use your notes from your discussion with your partner.

Step 3. Edit

a. Read your paragraph. Can you find any problems? Use the Editing Checklist.
b. Ask your partner to use the Peer Editing Checklist.

Step 4. Publish

a. Correct any problems in your paragraph. Use the Editing Checklist and the Peer Editing Checklist to help you.
b. Copy the paragraph in your best handwriting.
c. Explain the changes in your paragraph to your partner.
d. Read your paragraph to the class.
e. Hang up your paragraph in the classroom.

Activity Book
Page 80

Review

Student
CD-ROM

VOCABULARY I can read and spell these words.

Words

bottom   middle   top

Meals

breakfast   dinner   lunch

Food

beef bacon	chicken	peas	rice	soup
beans	eggs	pizza	salad	steak
cereal	hamburger	potatoes	sandwich	toast

Place settings

bowl	glass	napkin	spoon
fork	knife	plate	tablecloth

GRAMMAR I can use this grammar.

Count and Noncount Nouns

count nouns:	an apple	a bowl	three bananas
noncount nouns:	fruit	rice	milk

WORD STUDY I can spell plural count nouns.

Plural Count Nouns

singular		**plural**
fork	⟶	forks
sandwich	⟶	sandwiches
cherry	⟶	cherries

Assess

VOCABULARY

Review pages 122–124.

1. I eat ____ at 7:30 AM.

   a. lunch   **b.** breakfast   **c.** morning   **d.** dinner

2. ____ is his favorite meat.

   a. Milk   **b.** Rice   **c.** Chicken   **d.** Soup

3. We cut steak with a ____ .

   a. fork   **b.** spoon   **c.** knife   **d.** napkin

GRAMMAR

Review page 125.

1. We want ____ .

   a. a rice   **b.** two rices   **c.** rice

2. Bananas are my favorite ____ .

   a. fruit   **b.** fruits   **c.** a fruit

3. He gives the children ____ .

   a. milks   **b.** milk   **c.** three milks

WORD STUDY What is the plural form of the noun?

Review page 126.

1. spoon   **a.** spoons   **b.** spoonz   **c.** spoones

2. potato   **a.** potatos   **b.** potatoes   **c.** potatohs

3. baby   **a.** babys   **b.** babies   **c.** babeis

Projects

Project 1: Make a Food Pyramid Poster

Work with a small group to make a food pyramid poster.

1. Brainstorm a list of foods for each food group.
2. Draw a large food pyramid on a piece of poster paper.
3. Find and cut out pictures of foods for each food group. Use old magazines, newspapers, or supermarket flyers. You can also draw pictures of the foods.
4. Classify the pictures by food groups. Paste your pictures on the correct part of the pyramid. Label the foods.
5. Hang the poster up in your classroom.

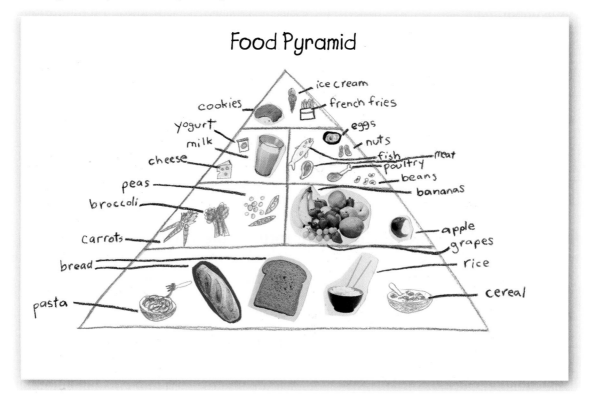

Project 2: Make a Class Recipe Book

Collect recipes to make a class recipe book.

1. Choose your favorite dish or a dish from your culture.
2. On a piece of paper, write your name and the name of your dish.
3. Write a list of the ingredients in the dish.
4. Write instructions (directions) for making the dish.
5. Draw a picture or paste a photo of the dish next to your recipe.
6. Put all of the class recipes together.
7. Make a cover for your class recipe book.
8. Make copies of the book for every student in your class.
9. Choose a dish in the book. Make the dish at home!

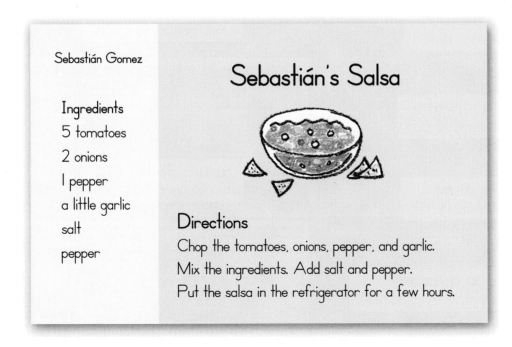

Sebastián Gomez

Sebastián's Salsa

Ingredients
5 tomatoes
2 onions
1 pepper
a little garlic
salt
pepper

Directions
Chop the tomatoes, onions, pepper, and garlic.
Mix the ingredients. Add salt and pepper.
Put the salsa in the refrigerator for a few hours.

Objectives

Listening and Speaking talking about money and prices

Grammar comparative adjectives

Word Study prefix re-

Reading myth

Writing opinion paragraph

Content Activity Book: math

Bills

a dollar bill
one dollar ($1.00)

a five dollar bill
five dollars ($5.00)

Coins

a penny
one cent ($.01)

a nickel
five cents ($.05)

a dime
ten cents ($.10)

a quarter
twenty-five cents ($.25)

a ten dollar bill
ten dollars ($10.00)

a twenty dollar bill
twenty dollars ($20.00)

Listen, Speak, Interact

Money and Prices

1 🎧 **Listen and repeat.** Listen and repeat the words and phrases.

2 **Pair work.** With your partner, find the right group of bills and coins to pay for the item.

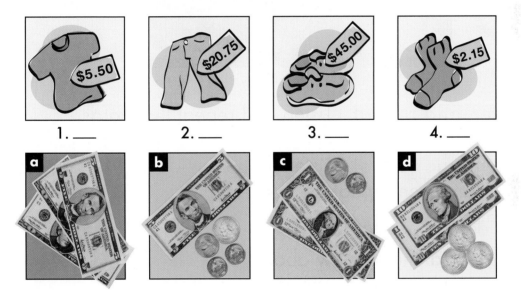

1. ___   2. ___   3. ___   4. ___

3 🎧 **Listen and repeat.** Listen to the conversations. Repeat the conversations.

4 🎧 **Listen.** What prices do you hear?

1.   2.   3.   4.   5.

Build Vocabulary

How Do You Pay for It?

credit card

ATM card

cash

salesperson

price

customer

check

5 🎧 **Listen and repeat.** Listen and repeat the words.

6 🎧 **Listen and repeat.** Listen to the conversation. Then repeat the conversation.

A: How do you pay for CDs?

B: I pay with a check. How about you?

A: I pay with cash.

> Ways to Pay:
> with cash
> with a credit card
> with a check

7 **Pair work.** Brainstorm a list of things you buy. Talk about how you pay for each thing.

A: How do you pay for ___ ?

B: I pay ___ . How about you?

A: I pay ___ .

CDs

clothes

food

VISIONS

Activity Book
Page 81

Grammar Focus
Comparative Adjectives

Comparative Adjectives

adjectives with one syllable
    cheap   cheap**er**

adjectives with two or more syllables
    expensive   **more** expensive

Use **comparative adjectives**
to compare two things.

Comparative Spelling Rules:

For adjectives that end in -y (with one or two syllables),
change the -y to *i* and add -*er*:   *pretty* ⟶ *prettier*

For adjectives ending in one vowel and one consonant,
double the consonant and add -*er*:
  big ⟶ *bigger*

Words to Know

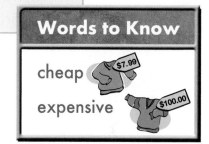

cheap

expensive

---

8 Choose. Read the adjective.
Choose the correct comparative form.

1. tall   **a.** taller   **b.** more tall

2. thin   **a.** thiner   **b.** thinner

3. happy   **a.** happier   **b.** happyer

4. important   **a.** more important   **b.** importanter

9 Compare. Which item is cheaper? Which is more expensive?

1. The milk is cheaper than the juice.

2. The juice is _____ than the milk.

3. The pants are _____ than the shirt.

4. The shirt is _____ than the pants.

Activity Book
Pages 82–83

Word Study

The Prefix *re-*

A **prefix** is a group of letters added to the beginning of a word. The word it is added to is called a **root word.** A prefix changes the meaning of the root word. The prefix *re-* means *again* or *back*.

Strategy

Word Recognition
Look for prefixes in new words. A prefix gives you information about the meaning of a word.

10 **Write a definition.** Look at each word. Find the prefix. Find the root word. Write a definition. Use a dictionary to check your definition.

1. reread: read again   **3.** review:

2. retell: **4.** rewrite:

11 **Unscramble.** Look at the cartoons. Unscramble the word under each of the cartoons.

1. perya repay   **2.** pnrteai ____   **3.** friell ____

Activity Book
Page 84

Into the Reading

Strategy

Preview Questions
Read the comprehension questions before the reading. This will help you know what information to look for as you read.

You will read a myth. The myth is about wishes and gold.

Use Prior Knowledge: What Do You Wish For?

A *wish* is something you want. What do you wish for? Do you wish for good health or happiness or good grades?

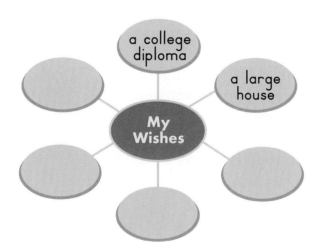

Build Background: Gold

Gold is a valuable yellow metal. Coins and jewelry are often made of gold.

Reading and Understanding

Text Structure: Myth

A **myth** is a made-up story. The characters often have special powers. Myths have a beginning, a middle, and an end. There are myths from many countries. The myth you will read is from Greece.

> A character is a person in a story.

Reading

King Midas and the Golden Touch

A king named Midas helps a man with special powers. The man is thankful. He tells Midas to make a wish. Midas wishes for the golden touch. Midas wants everything he touches to turn to gold. Midas thinks this is an excellent wish.

Midas gets his wish. He touches a chair. It turns to gold. He touches a table. It turns to gold. Everything he touches turns to gold! Midas is very happy.

Midas becomes hungry. He picks up a piece of meat. But he can't eat it because it turns to gold. He picks up a piece of bread. The bread turns to gold. Midas says, "I'll starve! Maybe my wish is not a good wish after all."

Midas's daughter is sad for her father. She hugs him. She turns to gold. Midas says, "The golden touch is a terrible thing! I was happier before. I don't want the golden touch anymore!" Midas goes to a river and cries. His tears wash away the golden touch.

Beyond the Reading

Reading comprehension. Answer the questions.

1. Does Midas wish for the golden touch?
2. Does Midas turn a chair or a bed to gold?
3. Who does Midas turn to gold?
4. Why doesn't he want the golden touch at the end of the story?

Make a story timeline.

a. Put the events of the story in order:

___ The man tells Midas to make a wish.

___ Midas washes away the golden touch with his tears.

___ Midas wishes for the golden touch.

___ Midas turns food and his daughter to gold. He is not happy.

1 Midas helps a man with special powers.

___ Midas turns objects to gold. He is happy.

b. Copy the story map. Put the events in the right boxes.

Beginning	Middle	End
1.	3.	5.
2.	4.	6.

Activity Book
Page 85–86

Retell the story. Use the story map to tell the events in the story.

From Reading to Writing

Is Money Important?

An opinion paragraph tells your feelings and beliefs about something. Write an opinion paragraph about money: Do you think money is important? Do you think it is not important?

> **Money Is Not Very Important**
>
> In my opinion, money is not very important. Money can help you buy things you want. But there are things that are more important than money. Money can't buy good health. Money can't buy love. Money is important, but it is not the most important thing.
>
> Svetlana Ivanova

Phrases for Expressing Opinions
I think...
I believe...
I feel that...
In my opinion...

Step 1. Plan

a. Think about money. What can you buy with money? What can't you buy with money?
b. Copy the chart. Make a list.

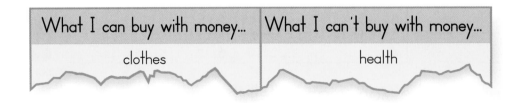

What I can buy with money...	What I can't buy with money...
clothes	health

VISIONS

Activity Book
Page 87

Step 2. Write

Write an opinion paragraph about the importance of money.

a. Write your opinion in your topic sentence.

b. Give reasons for your opinion in your detail sentences. Use notes from your chart.

Step 3. Edit

a. Read your paragraph. Can you find any problems? Use the Editing Checklist.

b. Ask your partner to use the Peer Editing Checklist.

Step 4. Publish

a. Correct any problems in your paragraph. Use the Editing Checklist and the Peer Editing Checklist to help you.

b. Copy the paragraph in your best handwriting or use a computer.

c. Explain the changes in your paragraph to your partner. Read your paragraph to the class.

Editing Checklist

☐ The sentences are in a paragraph.

☐ My paragraph begins with a topic sentence.

☐ My paragraph includes details about the topic sentence.

☐ I expressed my opinion in the paragraph.

Peer Editing Checklist

☐ I see the topic sentence.

☐ I see details about the topic sentence.

☐ I understand my partner's opinion.

Do you see any problems in the paragraph?_____
_____

Activity Book
Page 88

Review

Student
CD-ROM

VOCABULARY I can read and spell these words.

| ATM card | character | check | customer | price |
| cash | cheap | credit card | expensive | salesperson |

Coins and bills

| a penny | a dime | a dollar | ten dollars |
| a nickel | a quarter | five dollars | twenty dollars |

Expressions

| I think... | I believe... | I feel that... | In my opinion... |

GRAMMAR I can use this grammar.

Comparative Adjectives

adjectives with one syllable: cheap   cheap**er**

adjectives with two or more syllables: expensive   **more** expensive

WORD STUDY I can identify and understand the prefix *re-*.

Prefix: *re-*

<u>re</u><u>tell</u>: tell again   <u>re</u><u>fill</u>: fill again

    ↓   ↓   ↓   ↓

prefix root word   prefix root word

Assess

VOCABULARY

Review pages 136–138.

1. We get cash from the ____ .

   a. store   **b.** salesperson   **c.** ATM machine   **d.** police officer

2. The ____ of the shirt is $15.99.

   a. money   **b.** cash   **c.** check   **d.** price

3. Three ____ is $.75.

   a. a quarter   **b.** five dollars   **c.** quarters   **d.** a dime

GRAMMAR

Review page 139.

1. I am ____ than my sister.

   a. short   **b.** more short   **c.** shorter   **d.** shortter

2. The kitchen is ____ than the living room.

   a. more big   **b.** more bigger   **c.** biger   **d.** bigger

3. The sofa is ____ than the table.

   a. expensiver   **b.** more expensive   **c.** expensive   **d.** very expensive

WORD STUDY

Review page 140.

1. In the word *review*, what is the prefix?

   a. review   **b.** re   **c.** view   **d.** ew

2. In the word *review*, what is the root word?

   a. re   **b.** review   **c.** view   **d.** noun

Projects

Project 1: Make a Menu

Work with a small group to make a restaurant menu.

1. Decide what kind of restaurant you want to open.
2. Create a name for your restaurant.
3. Brainstorm a list of foods for your menu.
4. Agree on the price of each food.
5. Create a menu. Use different fonts and art to make your menu interesting. Make sure to include:
   a. the name of the restaurant
   b. the food items
   c. the price of each food item
6. Hang up your menu in the classroom.

Alfonso's Italian Restaurant

Lunch

slice of pizza	$1.95
calzone	$2.50
sandwich	$4.25
soup	$2.25

Dinner

spaghetti and meatballs	$7.95
lasagna	$8.95
pasta and chicken	$8.95
vegetarian pasta	$6.50
garlic bread	$1.50

Project 2: Create a Store

Work with a small group to create a store.

1. Decide what kind of store you want to open.
2. Make a sign for your store. Hang it up on the wall behind your group.
3. What items will your store sell? Find a picture of each item in old newspapers or magazines, or draw a picture of each item. Hang the pictures up.
4. Decide how much each item costs. Write a list of the items and prices.
5. Open your store! One or two students in your group can be the salespeople. The others can be customers in your classmates' stores. Take turns.
6. Shop in your classmates' stores. Pretend you have $20.00. Decide what items you want to buy.

Useful Phrases
Customer: Excuse me.
How much is/are (item[s])?
Salesperson: It's (price).
Customer: Thank you.

Jobs

cashier A cashier takes money and gives change.

chef A chef prepares food.

firefighter A firefighter puts out fires.

child-care worker A child-care worker takes care of children.

doctor A doctor takes care of sick people.

hairstylist A hairstylist cuts hair.

Listen, Speak, Interact

What's the Job?

1 🎧 **Listen and repeat.** Listen and repeat the words and sentences.

2 🎧 **Listen and identify.** What job do you hear?

1. chef / cashier / hairstylist
2. doctor / hairstylist / firefighter
3. doctor / cashier / child-care worker
4. child-care worker / firefighter / chef
5. firefighter / doctor / hairstylist

3 **Pair work.** Look at the jobs on page 150. Choose one. Act it out for your partner. Your partner will guess the job.

4 **Group work.** What other jobs do you know? Brainstorm a list of jobs. Ask your teacher for help or use a bilingual dictionary.

Build Vocabulary

Job Tools and Objects

Choices
by Jill Korey O Sullivan

There are so many things I'd like to do.
I'm considering some jobs. Here are a few:

I'd like to be an astronaut and wear a special suit.
I'd like to be a musician. Perhaps I'll play the flute.

Maybe I'll be a waiter and serve food on a tray.
Maybe I'll be an artist and work with paint or clay.

I'd like to be a mechanic and fix cars with a wrench.
Or perhaps I'll teach English. Or maybe even French.

I could be a carpenter and use a hammer and nails.
Or a grocery store clerk who weighs things on scales.

Hey, I know what I should be. I know the perfect
    job for me:
A job that's interesting every day—president
    of the USA!

5 🎧 Listen. Listen to the poem.

6 Categorize. Copy the chart below. Reread the poem.
Put the jobs and the tools in the columns of the chart.

Job	Tools
musician	flute

Activity Book
Page 89

Grammar Focus

Object Pronouns

Pronouns are words used in place of nouns. Use **object pronouns** after a verb or a preposition.

Object Pronouns	Subject	Verb	Object
me	You	like	me.
you	I	like	you.
him	I	like	him.
her	I	like	her.
it	I	like	it.
us	He	likes	us.
them	I	like	them.

After a verb:

Maria is my neighbor. I know **her** well.
  ↓   ↓
 noun   object pronoun

After a preposition:

He is in my class. I often eat lunch with **him**.
 ↓   ↓
noun   object pronoun

> With, at, and to are prepositions.

7 Complete the sentence. Finish the sentences with an object pronoun.

1. She is my best friend. I really like <u>her</u> .

2. My parents cook every night. Sometimes I help ___ .

3. John and I are in the same class. He usually sits next to ___ .

4. This is my favorite TV program. I watch ___ every week.

5. My grandfather lives in Florida. I visit ___ every summer.

VISIONS

Activity Book
Pages 90–91

Word Study

The Suffix -er

A **suffix** is a group of letters added to the end of a root word. A suffix changes the meaning of the root word. The suffix -er means *someone who does something*.

> **Strategy**
>
> Word Recognition
> Look for suffixes in new words. A suffix gives you information about the meaning of a word.

8 Write a definition. Look at each word. Find the root word. Look it up in a dictionary, if necessary. Find the suffix. Write a definition.

> Add -er to the end of most verbs: work → worker
>
> For verbs that end in e, drop the e before you add -er: write → writer

1. painter: someone who paints

2. writer:

3. gardener:

4. manager:

9 Match. Add the suffix -er to each root word in the box. Match the new words to the pictures.

paint	dance	sing	teach

1. singer

2. _____

3. _____

4. _____

VISIONS

Activity Book
Page 92

Into the Reading

You will read an article about how to take a fast-food order.

Use Prior Knowledge: How Do You Order Fast Food?

How do you order food at a fast-food restaurant? What do you do first? What do you do second? Make a list.

Ordering Fast Food	
1. I look at the menu.	4.
2. I choose the items I want.	5.
3.	6.

Build Background: Cash Registers

A cash register usually has keys with numbers. Cashiers use the keys to punch in prices. Cash registers at fast-food restaurants often have words or pictures of the items on the keys instead of numbers.

Reading and Understanding

Text Structure: "How-To" Narration

A **"how-to" narration** explains how to do something. It explains the steps you need to take. It gives these steps in sequence. Reading a "how-to" narration can teach you how to do something.

🎧 Reading

How to Take a Fast-Food Order

My name is Alex. I work in a fast-food restaurant. I stand behind the counter and take orders from customers. This is how I take an order:

First, the customer comes in and tells me what he wants. Then, I press the buttons on the cash register for the items the customer orders. After that, I tell him how much the order costs. The customer gives me money. I put it in the cash register. Sometimes I need to give the customer change. Next, I call out the order to my coworkers. Finally, my coworkers bring the food to the counter, and I put it on the tray. Then, I'm ready for the next customer.

I like my job. I meet a lot of nice people, and I get a lot of free lunches!

Beyond the Reading

Reading comprehension. Answer the questions.

1. Does Alex work in a fast-food restaurant?
2. Does Alex cook or take orders at the counter?
3. Who brings the food to the counter?
4. How does Alex feel about his job?

Illustrate the order of events. Reread the "how-to" narration. How does the writer take a fast-food order? Think about the sequence of events. On a piece of paper, draw a picture of each step in taking a fast-food order. Draw the pictures in the right sequence.

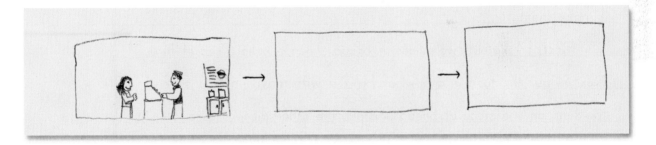

Retell the sequence of events. Use your drawings to explain to your partner how to take a fast-food order.

Act out the sequence of events. Act out the sequence of events with your partner. One of you should be the fast-food worker. The other should be the customer.

Activity Book
Pages 93–94

From Reading to Writing

A "How-To" Paragraph

Write a "how-to" paragraph. Explain how to do something. Include all of the steps in sequence. Here are some possible subjects to write about:

Use **sequence words** to tell the order things happen in:

first	next	finally
after	then	

- how to make a telephone call
- how to use a microwave
- how to play soccer
- how to make a sandwich

How to Make a Tuna Sandwich

Tuna sandwiches are my favorite kind of sandwich. This is how I make them:

First, I take out two pieces of bread. Then, I open a can of tuna. Next, I put the tuna in a bowl and mix it with mayonnaise. I spread the tuna on one piece of bread and put the other piece of bread on top of it. Finally, I eat it, of course!

Reiko Toshimoyo

Step 1. Plan

a. Choose an activity you know how to do.
b. Think about the steps for doing this activity.
c. Write a list of the steps. Make sure the steps are in sequence.

Activity Book
Page 95

Step 2. Write

Write a paragraph about how to do your activity. Use the ideas from your list. Use sequence words in your paragraph.

Step 3. Edit

a. Read your paragraph. Can you find any problems? Use the Editing Checklist.
b. Ask your partner to use the Peer Editing Checklist.

Step 4. Publish

a. Correct any problems in your paragraph. Use the Editing Checklist and the Peer Editing Checklist to help you.
b. Copy the paragraph in your best handwriting or use a computer.
c. Explain the changes in your paragraph to your partner.
d. Collect all your classmates' articles. Make a class "how-to" book. Draw a cover for the book.
e. Give each student in your class a copy. Share the book with another class.

Editing Checklist

☐ The sentences are in a paragraph.

☐ My paragraph explains how to do something.

☐ All the steps are in order.

☐ My paragraph includes sequence words.

Peer Editing Checklist

☐ The paragraph explains how to do something.

☐ The steps are clear.

☐ The writer uses sequence words correctly.

Do you see any problems in the paragraph?_____
_____

Activity Book
Page 96

Review

VOCABULARY I can read and spell these words.

Jobs

artist	child-care worker	mechanic
astronaut	doctor	musician
carpenter	firefighter	waiter
cashier	grocery store clerk	
chef	hairstylist	

Job tools and objects

clay	nails	thermometer
flute	scales	tray
hammer	scissors	wrench

Sequence words

first	next	finally
after	then	

GRAMMAR I can use this grammar.

Object Pronouns

me	him	it	them
you	her	us	

WORD STUDY I can identify and understand the suffix -er.

Suffix: -er

singer

painter

Assess

VOCABULARY

Review pages 150–152.

1. The _____ takes orders and brings food to the tables.

   a. cashier   **b.** chef   **c.** waiter   **d.** farmer

2. The _____ fixes cars.

   a. carpenter   **b.** mechanic   **c.** police officer   **d.** hairstylist

3. The hairstylist cuts hair with _____ .

   a. scissors   **b.** a wrench   **c.** scales   **d.** a tractor

GRAMMAR

Review page 153.

1. He's a friendly person. I like _____ .

   a. her   **b.** him   **c.** you   **d.** me

2. The movie is great. You should see _____ .

   a. them   **b.** us   **c.** it   **d.** her

3. We are going to a movie. Do you want to come with _____ ?

   a. us   **b.** them   **c.** it   **d.** him

WORD STUDY

Review page 154.

1. In the word *singer*, what is the suffix?

   a. si   **b.** singer   **c.** er   **d.** ger

2. In the word *singer*, what is the root word?

   a. si   **b.** sing   **c.** er   **d.** ger

Projects

Project 1: Invite a Guest Speaker to Class

Invite a person from your community to come to your class
to speak about his or her job.

1. With your class, brainstorm some interesting jobs in your community, like mail carrier, police officer, or firefighter.
2. Vote on the job that the most students want to learn about.
3. Write a letter to a person in your community with this job. Explain that your class is interested in learning about the job. Invite the person to your class to speak about his or her job.
4. Before the person comes to visit, prepare a list of questions to ask.
5. Listen to the speaker. Take notes on information you learn.
6. When the speaker is finished speaking, ask questions.
7. Make sure to thank the guest speaker.

Dear Mr. Jakes,

We are a 10th grade class at East Hill High School. We are studying different jobs. We are very interested in learning more about the job of a firefighter. We hope you or another firefighter from your fire station can come visit our class and tell us about your job.

Sincerely,

Ms. Chen's 10th grade class

Project 2: Give a "How-To" Presentation

Give a how-to presentation.

1. Choose an activity you know how to do.
2. What are the steps for doing this activity?
   Write notes on the sequence of the steps.
3. Gather any objects that will help your presentation,
   or draw a poster with pictures of the objects.
4. Practice your presentation.
5. Give your presentation. Make sure you:
   a. use your notes
   b. use the objects
   c. speak clearly
   d. speak slowly
   e. make eye contact with your classmates
6. Evaluate your presentation with this checklist.

Presentation Checklist
☐ I used my notes.
☐ I used objects.
☐ I spoke clearly.
☐ I spoke slowly.
☐ I made eye contact.

CHAPTER 9 Holidays

Objectives

Listening and Speaking talking about holidays

Grammar past tense: *be* and regular verbs

Word Study consonant clusters: *s* blends

Reading biography

Writing autobiography

Content Activity Book: social studies

Valentine's Day

flowers

chocolates

heart

I love you!

card

Fourth of July

fireworks

barbecue

parade

Thanksgiving

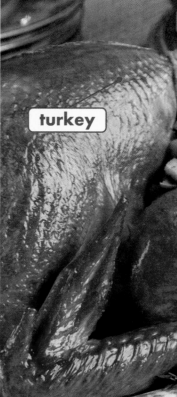

pie

turkey

stuffing

Listen, Speak, Interact

What's the Holiday?

1 🎧 **Listen and repeat.** Listen and repeat the words.

2 🎧 **Listen and identify.** What holiday do you hear?

1. Fourth of July / Thanksgiving / Valentine's Day
2. Fourth of July / Thanksgiving / Valentine's Day
3. Fourth of July / Thanksgiving / Valentine's Day

3 **Group work.** What other holidays do you know? Brainstorm a list of holidays. Include holidays from different cultures.

4 **Pair work.** Ask your partner about his or her favorite holiday. Find out the name of the holiday and how your partner celebrates it.

Build Vocabulary

Holidays Throughout the Year

5 🎧 **Listen and repeat.** Listen and repeat the holidays.

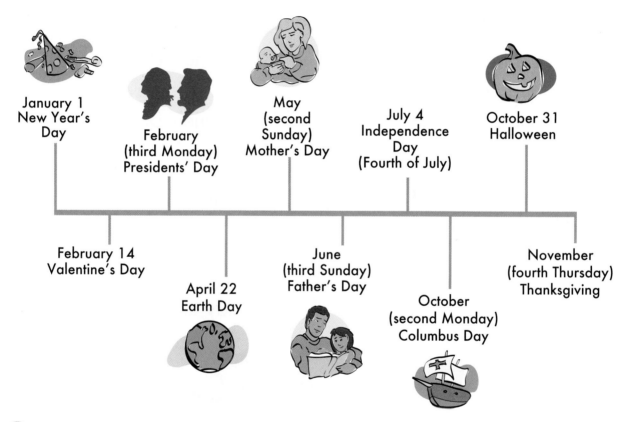

January 1
New Year's
Day

February
(third Monday)
Presidents' Day

May
(second
Sunday)
Mother's Day

July 4
Independence
Day
(Fourth of July)

October 31
Halloween

February 14
Valentine's Day

April 22
Earth Day

June
(third Sunday)
Father's Day

October
(second Monday)
Columbus Day

November
(fourth Thursday)
Thanksgiving

6 **What's missing?** Copy the timeline. Can you think of other holidays celebrated in the United States? Add as many holidays to the timeline as you can.

7 **Pair work.** Do you know any holidays from other cultures? Tell your partner about the holidays. Add the holidays to the timeline.

Activity Book
Page 97

Grammar Focus

Past Tense: *be* and Regular Verbs

Use the **past tense** to tell about an action in the past.

Past Tense of *be*	Past Tense of Regular Verbs
I **was** sick yesterday.	I work**ed** yesterday.
You **were** sick yesterday.	You stud**ied** yesterday.
He **was** sick yesterday.	He cook**ed** yesterday.
She **was** sick yesterday.	She exercis**ed** yesterday.
It **was** sick yesterday.	It play**ed** yesterday.
We **were** sick yesterday.	We danc**ed** yesterday.
They **were** sick yesterday.	They paint**ed** yesterday.

8 **Complete the sentences.** Add *was* or *were* to each sentence.

Our Fourth of July barbecue ¹<u>was</u> fun. We ²____ with all of our friends. Maria ³____ there with her brother. Thomas ⁴____ the cook. The fireworks ⁵____ beautiful. It ⁶____ a great day!

9 **Rewrite.** Make the sentences past tense.

1. My parents cook Thanksgiving dinner.
2. I order an apple pie from the bakery.
3. We finish the pie.
4. My parents ask for the recipe.

Activity Book
Pages 98–99

Word Study

Consonant Clusters: s blends

Often when *s* and another consonant are together in a word, the sounds of the letters are blended together.

Consonant Clusters: *s* blends	
s + *p* = *sp*:	speak, spell, spend, sport
s + *t* = *st*:	student, start, study, story
s + *k* = *sk*:	skate, skip, ski, skin

10 🎧 **Listen and repeat.** Listen to the sounds the two consonants make separately and together. Then listen to the blend in each word. Repeat each word.

11 🎧 **Read and listen.** Read and listen to the poem. Then find the words in the poem with the *sp, st,* and *sk* blends.

12 **Pair work.** Take turns reading the poem with a partner.

> **Fourth of July Night**
> *by Eleanor Dennis*
>
> The fireworks are a lot of fun.
> I watch each giant spark
> As it goes streaking up the sky—
> Then lights up all the dark
> In a lovely splashing splatter
> Of a thousand silver stars,
> In a tumbling, rumbling clatter
> That goes echoing off to Mars.

13 **What is the missing blend?** Complete the word with *sp, st,* or *sk.*

1. <u>st</u> ar

2. __ oon

3. __ airs

4. __ irt

Activity Book
Page 100

Into the Reading

You will read a biography of a famous American leader, Martin Luther King Jr.

Use Prior Knowledge: Leaders

A leader is a person who directs other people. There are many kinds of leaders. There are leaders of countries, companies, teams, and other groups. Sometimes a leader is a person who organizes and leads people who share a goal.

Make a list of leaders. Set up a chart like the one below. In one column, write the leader's name. In the other column, write what the person leads.

Leader	Leader of...
Miguel	our soccer team
Janet Romero	our city

Build Background: Peaceful Protest

In the United States, people have freedom of speech. They can protest things they think are wrong or unfair. A protest is a way of showing disagreement. A peaceful protest is a calm, quiet protest with no violence or trouble. Martin Luther King Jr. led peaceful protests.

Reading and Understanding

Text Structure: Biography

A **biography** is a true story about a person's life. The story is written by someone else. Biographies include important dates and events in the person's life.

Reading

Martin Luther King Jr.: American Leader

Martin Luther King Jr. was a great American leader. He was born on January 15, 1929, in Atlanta, Georgia. His father was a minister and his mother was a teacher. He liked to play baseball and sing in his father's church. He was an excellent student. He graduated from college in 1948. On June 18, 1953, he married Coretta Scott. In 1954, he started work as a minister.

Dr. King lived at a time when black and white Americans did not have equal rights everywhere. Dr. King wanted all people to be treated the same. Dr. King organized peaceful protests against unequal treatment. He did not fight. He wanted to change the laws peacefully. He was successful. He helped bring equality and understanding to all Americans. In 1964, he accepted the Nobel Peace Prize.

On April 4, 1968, someone killed Dr. King with a gunshot. In November 1983, the United States Congress created Martin Luther King Jr. Day. This national holiday honors Dr. King and his work. Martin Luther King Jr. Day is the third Monday in January.

Beyond the Reading

Reading comprehension. Answer the questions.

1. Was Martin Luther King Jr. born in 1928?
2. Was his father a minister or a teacher?
3. What prize did Dr. King accept?
4. What did Dr. King believe?

Fill in a timeline.

A timeline lists events in the order that they happened.

a. Fill in the missing information on the timeline of Martin Luther King Jr.'s life.

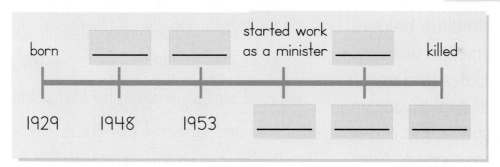

b. Work with a partner. Use the timeline to ask and answer questions about Martin Luther King Jr.'s life. Ask questions like:
   • When was Martin Luther King Jr. born?
   • When did he graduate from college?
   • What happened in 1953?

Draw a picture. Draw a picture of one of the events in Martin Luther King Jr.'s life. Show the picture to your class. Explain the picture.

Activity Book
Pages 101–102

From Reading to Writing

Write an Autobiography

An **autobiography** is the story of a person's life. The person the story is about is also the writer of the story. Write an autobiography of your life in one or two paragraphs.

Step 1. Plan

a. Think about the important events in your life.

b. Copy the timeline below.

c. Fill in the timeline with the important dates and events in your life. Make sure you list the events in the order that they happened. Add more lines to the timeline if necessary.

My Life

I was born in 1992 in Haiti. My family lived in Port-au-Prince. This is Haiti's capital city. We lived in an apartment near the center of the city. In 1993, my little sister was born.

Then, in 1997, we moved to the United States and I started elementary school here. I started middle school in 2003. In 2004, I joined the basketball team. I love this sport.

I am very happy in the United States. I like my school and I have a lot of friends. I'm glad my family moved here.

Marie Faustin

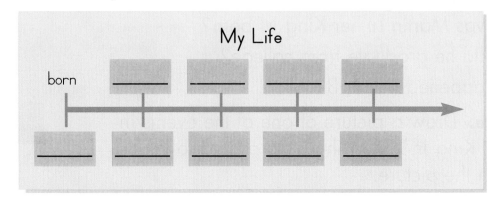

Activity Book
Page 103

Step 2. Write

Write a one- or two-paragraph autobiography. Use the dates and events from your timeline.

Step 3. Edit

a. Read your autobiography. Can you find any problems? Use the Editing Checklist.
b. Ask your partner to use the Peer Editing Checklist.

Step 4. Publish

a. Correct any problems in your paragraph. Use the Editing Checklist and the Peer Editing Checklist to help you.
b. Copy the autobiography in your best handwriting or use a computer.
c. Explain the changes in your autobiography to your partner.
d. Attach one or two pictures from important events in your life to your autobiography.
e. Hang up your autobiography in the class.

Editing Checklist

☐ My autobiography tells about events and dates in my life.

☐ I used the past tense correctly.

☐ The spelling and punctuation are correct.

Peer Editing Checklist

☐ The autobiography tells about the events and dates in the writer's life.

☐ The writer uses the past tense correctly.

☐ The spelling and punctuation are correct.

Do you see any problems in the paragraph? _____

_____

VISIONS

Activity Book
Page 104

Review

Student
CD-ROM

VOCABULARY I can read and spell these words.

barbecue	chocolates	flowers	parade	stuffing
card	fireworks	heart	pie	turkey

Holidays

Columbus Day	Independence Day	Presidents' Day
Earth Day	Martin Luther King Jr. Day	Thanksgiving
Father's Day	Mother's Day	Valentine's Day
Halloween	New Year's Day	

GRAMMAR I can use this grammar.

Past Tense: *be* and Regular Verbs

Past Tense of *be*

I/He/She/It **was** late yesterday.

You/We/They **were** late yesterday.

Past Tense of Regular Verbs

I/You/He/She work**ed** yesterday.

It/We/They

WORD STUDY I can recognize and say these blends.

Consonant Clusters: *s* Blends

s + p = sp:	**sp**eak, **sp**ill, **sp**end
s + t = st:	**st**and, **st**art, **st**ate
s + k = sk:	**sk**ate, **sk**i, **sk**im

Assess

VOCABULARY

Review pages 164–166.

1. I always give my sister a _____ on her birthday.

    a. stuffing   **b.** card   **c.** parade   **d.** Thanksgiving

2. Most countries celebrate _____ on January 1.

    a. Earth Day   **b.** Mother's Day   **c.** New Year's Day   **d.** Columbus Day

3. _____ is my favorite meat.

    a. Pie   **b.** Stuffing   **c.** Pizza   **d.** Turkey

GRAMMAR

Review page 167.

1. They ____ home yesterday.

    a. is   **b.** are   **c.** was   **d.** were

2. I ____ dinner last night.

    a. was   **b.** cook   **c.** were   **d.** cooked

3. My friend ____ in Mexico last year.

    a. lives   **b.** lived   **c.** live   **d.** liveed

WORD STUDY

Review page 168.

Which consonant cluster does the object begin with?

1.   **a.** st   **b.** sp   **c.** sk   **d.** s

2.   **a.** sp   **b.** st   **c.** so   **d.** st

Projects

Project 1: American Holiday Presentation

Give a presentation about an American holiday.

1. Choose an American holiday you want to know more about.
2. Make a list of questions about the holiday. For example:
   - When is the holiday?
   - What does the holiday celebrate?
   - Do people wear special clothes on this holiday?
     If yes, what kind of clothes?
   - Do people eat special food on this holiday?
     If yes, what kind of food?
   - Do people give cards or gifts on this holiday?
3. Discuss your questions with American teachers, friends, and neighbors. Take notes on what you learn.
4. Gather any objects that will help your presentation, or draw a poster with pictures of the objects.
5. Practice your presentation.
6. Give your presentation.
   Make sure you:
   a. use your notes
   b. use the objects
   c. speak clearly
   d. speak slowly
   e. make eye contact with your classmates
7. Evaluate your presentation with this checklist.

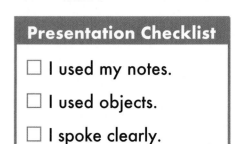

Presentation Checklist
☐ I used my notes.
☐ I used objects.
☐ I spoke clearly.
☐ I spoke slowly.
☐ I made eye contact.

Project 2: Timeline of a Famous American's Life

Research the life of a famous American and create a timeline of the person's life.

1. Choose a famous American you want to learn more about.
2. Go to your school or local library. Ask the librarian to help you find short and simple biographies of the famous American.
3. Scan the biographies. Write down the important dates and events in the person's life.
4. Draw a large timeline on a piece of poster paper.
5. Fill in the important dates and events of the person's life in the timeline.
6. Draw pictures or paste photographs next to some of the events to illustrate the events.
7. Hang up your timeline in class.

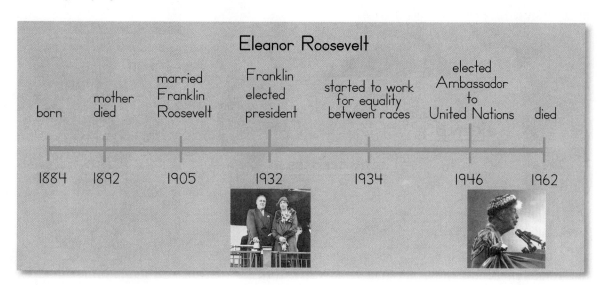

Eleanor Roosevelt

born	mother died	married Franklin Roosevelt	Franklin elected president	started to work for equality between races	elected Ambassador to United Nations	died
1884	1892	1905	1932	1934	1946	1962

CHAPTER 10

Feelings

Objectives

Listening and Speaking talking about feelings

Grammar future tense with *will*

Word Study long and short vowel review

Reading poem

Writing personal letter

Content Activity Book: science

shy

scared

happy

mad

bored

sad

excited

surprised

embarrassed

Listen, Speak, Interact

How Do You Feel?

1 🎧 **Listen and repeat.** Listen and repeat the words.

2 🎧 **Listen and identify.**
How does the person feel?
1. shy / scared / surprised
2. embarrassed / happy / mad
3. shy / bored / mad
4. surprised / scared / excited

3 Pair work. Look at the feelings on page 178. Choose four feelings. Act them out for your partner. Your partner will guess the feelings.

4 Group work. What other feelings can you think of? Brainstorm a list of feelings. Ask your teacher for help or use a bilingual dictionary.

Build Vocabulary

When I'm Happy, I Smile

5 🎧 **Listen and repeat.** Listen and repeat the words.

 smile shout shake blush

6 🎧 **Fill in the blanks.** Complete the sentences with actions from the box.

 jump laugh cry  yawn

| jump | shout | shake | yawn |
| cry | laugh | blush | smile |

1. When I'm excited, I jump .

2. When I'm sad, I ___ .

3. When I'm bored, I ___ .

4. When I'm embarrassed, I ___ .

5. When I'm scared, I ___ .

6. When I'm happy, I ___ .

7. When I'm happy, I also ___ .

8. When I'm angry, I ___ .

Activity Book
Page 105

Grammar Focus

Future Tense with *will*

I	will	go.
You	will	go.
He	will	go.
She	will	go.
It	will	go.
We	will	go.
They	will	go.

The **future tense** tells about events that will happen in the future.

7 **Choose.** Which sentences are true about your future?

1. I will cook dinner tonight.
   I will not cook dinner tonight.
2. I will rent a movie tonight.
   I will not rent a movie tonight.
3. I'll come to school tomorrow.
   I won't come to school tomorrow.
4. I'll be a senior next year.
   I won't be a senior next year.

Contractions
I'll, you'll, he'll, she'll, it'll, we'll, they'll

Negative
will not = won't

8 **Write.** Change each sentence to a future tense sentence.

1. Mario called his friend.
2. We go to the library.
3. You rented a movie.
4. She was bored.
5. We eat lunch at 12:00.
6. The cat sleeps here.

9 **Write.** Write three true future tense sentences. Use contractions.

I'll have lunch with my friend today.

I won't watch TV tonight.

I'll study for my test tonight.

Activity Book
Pages 106–107

Word Study

Long and Short Vowel Review

10 Choose. Which is the right vowel sound?

1. long e / short e

2. long i / short i

3. long a / short a

4. long o / short o

5. long u / short u

6. long i / short i

7. long e / short e

8. long a / short a

11 Listen. Do these words rhyme?

1. run, sun   **3.** lip, rip   **5.** leave, life

2. bag, big   **4.** pay, day   **6.** way, say

12 Pair work. Say the following rhyming word pairs. Think of another word that rhymes with each pair. (Hint: You can find rhyming words in the Activity 10 pictures.)

1. cat, bat, _hat_   **3.** ten, then, ____

2. dish, wish, ____   **4.** take, bake, ____

Activity Book
Page 108

Into the Reading

You will read a poem. In the poem, a girl tells her feelings about starting a new school.

Use Prior Knowledge: Feelings About the First Day of School

How did you feel before your first day of school? Copy the word web onto a piece of paper. Fill it in with the feelings you had before your first day of school.

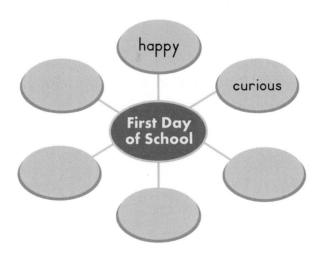

Build Background: Monsters

Monsters are ugly creatures that scare people. Monsters are not real. They are only in people's imaginations. Children are often scared of monsters.

Reading and Understanding

Text Structure: Poem

Poems often tell about feelings. Look for the feelings the writer expresses in this poem.

Reading

Patti Bennett
a poem by Mel Glenn

Papa, when I was six,
You came into my room and scared away the monsters.
I still want you to come into my room and
Scare away the doubts I have about starting high school.
You say I'll do all right.
I say I'm scared silly.
You say the teachers will all love me.
I say how will they know who I am?
You say I'm a big girl now.
I say I'm only fourteen years old.
Papa, I'd like you to tell me
Everything's going to be all right,
That I'll make new friends,
That I'll get a high average,
That I will be able to find my own way.
Papa, is this outfit OK?
Oh, you have to say that.

Beyond the Reading

Reading comprehension. Answer the questions.

1. Does Patti want her father's help?

2. Is Patti starting middle school or high school?

3. How does Patti feel?

4. What does Patti want her father to say?

Strategy

Compare and Contrast
Compare and contrast your feelings and experiences with the feelings and experiences of the character in the reading. This can help you understand the reading better.

Compare and contrast. Were your feelings about starting school like Patti's? How were they the same? How were they different? Copy and complete the Venn Diagram. Fill it in with your own ideas.

Patti

Patti and Me

Me

worried scared excited

Activity Book
Pages 109–110

From Reading to Writing

A Personal Letter

Write a letter to a friend or relative. Tell how you feel about something new, exciting, or difficult happening in your life.

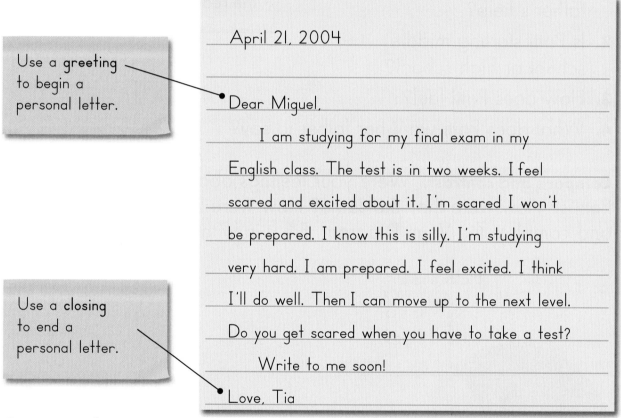

Use a greeting to begin a personal letter.

April 21, 2004

Dear Miguel,

   I am studying for my final exam in my English class. The test is in two weeks. I feel scared and excited about it. I'm scared I won't be prepared. I know this is silly. I'm studying very hard. I am prepared. I feel excited. I think I'll do well. Then I can move up to the next level. Do you get scared when you have to take a test?
   Write to me soon!
Love, Tia

Use a closing to end a personal letter.

Step 1. Plan

a. Think about the new, exciting, or difficult things happening in your life now or soon. Choose one of these things to write about.

b. Think about how you feel about this event. Choose a friend or relative to write a letter to about your feelings.

VISIONS

Activity Book
Page 111

Step 2. Write

Write a letter about the event you chose. Remember to include a greeting and a closing in your letter.

Step 3. Edit

a. Read your letter. Can you find any problems? Use the Editing Checklist.

b. Ask your partner to use the Peer Editing Checklist.

Step 4. Publish

a. Correct any problems in your letter. Use the Editing Checklist and the Peer Editing Checklist to help you.

b. Copy the letter in your best handwriting or use a computer.

c. Explain the changes in your paragraph to your partner.

d. Mail your letter to the person you wrote it to.

Editing Checklist

☐ My letter has a greeting and a closing.

☐ My letter tells about something new, exciting, or difficult happening in my life.

☐ I tell my feelings in the letter.

☐ The spelling and punctuation are correct.

Peer Editing Checklist

☐ The letter has a greeting and a closing.

☐ The letter tells about something new, exciting, or difficult happening in the writer's life.

☐ The letter tells about the writer's feelings.

☐ The spelling and punctuation are correct.

Do you see any problems in the paragraph? _____

_____

Activity Book
Page 112

Review

VOCABULARY I can read and spell these words.

Feeling adjectives

bored	happy	scared
embarrassed	mad	shy
excited	sad	surprised

Verbs

blush	jump	shake	smile
cry	laugh	shout	yawn

GRAMMAR I can use this grammar.

Future Tense with *will*

I / You / We / They	**will**	go.
He / She / It	**will**	go.

WORD STUDY I can recognize and say long and short vowel sounds.

Long and Short Vowels

cake   **cat**

long a   short a

Assess

VOCABULARY

1. He often feels _____ around new people.

   a. shy   **b.** mad   **c.** surprised   **d.** blush

2. I got an A on my exam! I'm so _____ .

   a. bored   **b.** mad   **c.** happy   **d.** shy

3. The movie is really sad. I'm sure you will _____ .

   a. shout   **b.** cry   **c.** laugh   **d.** shake

> Review pages 178–180.

GRAMMAR

1. He _____ dinner tonight.

   a. cooking   **b.** cook   **c.** will cook

2. I will _____ tonight.

   a. studying   **b.** studied   **c.** study

3. They _____ come to class tomorrow.

   a. will not   **b.** not will   **c.** not

> Review page 181.

WORD STUDY Choose the rhyming word.

1. lip   **a.** hip   **b.** sick   **c.** win

2. bag   **a.** sit   **b.** flag   **c.** bat

3. street   **a.** stop   **b.** meet   **c.** teeth

> Review page 182.

Projects

Project 1: Keep a Diary

A diary is a book in which you write about personal thoughts and feelings every day. Keep a diary for a week.

1. Create a diary. Staple together a few sheets of paper. Create a cover for your diary.
2. At the end of each day, find a quiet place to write in your diary. Write the date at the top of the page. Use letter-writing style to write in your diary. Begin with "Dear Diary,".
3. Think about the events of the day and how you felt about them. Write about your thoughts and feelings.
4. You can draw pictures or paste small objects from the day in your diary. This will help you remember the day.
5. Do this every day for a week. Then, bring your diary to class and read a portion from it to a classmate or the class. Do not read any part of the diary you do not want to share.

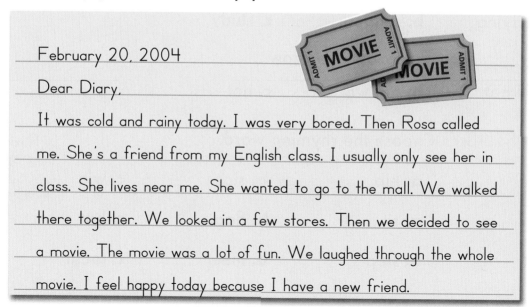

February 20, 2004

Dear Diary,

It was cold and rainy today. I was very bored. Then Rosa called me. She's a friend from my English class. I usually only see her in class. She lives near me. She wanted to go to the mall. We walked there together. We looked in a few stores. Then we decided to see a movie. The movie was a lot of fun. We laughed through the whole movie. I feel happy today because I have a new friend.

Project 2: Act It Out

Act out a situation with a partner.

1. With your partner, choose a feeling.

2. Think of a situation that would give you this feeling. You can use one of these examples or create a situation of your own:

happy: A friend gives you a present.

scared: You ask someone for directions to class on the first day of school.

mad: Your friend borrowed your jacket and lost it.

excited: You get tickets to a concert you want to see.

3. Write a dialogue for this play with your partner.

4. Practice the play with your partner. Use any costumes and objects that help your play.

5. Perform the play for the class.

6. The class will guess what emotion you are acting.

The 100 Most Frequently Used English Words

Many of these words do not follow the sound-symbol rules. You need to be able to recognize and spell these important words.

A

a
about
after
all
am
an
and
are
as
at

B

back
be
because
been
big
but
by

C

came
can
come
could

D

day
did
do
down

F

first
for
from

G

get
go
going
got

H

had
has
have
he
her
here
him
his

I

I
if
in
into
is
it

J

just

L

like
little
look

M

made
make
me
more
my

N

no
not
now

O

of
off
on
one
only
or
our
out
over

S

said
saw
see
she
so
some

T

that
the
their
them
then
there
they
this
to
two

U

up

V

very

W

was
we
well
went
were
what
when
where
which
who
will
with
would

Y

you
your

Learning Strategies

Tips to Help Me Learn

Metacognitive Strategies — Do I plan ahead and check as I learn?

1. **Advance Organizers** — What do the text features—the title, the section headings, the pictures—tell me about the subject?

2. **Selective Attention** — What will be the most important information to pay attention to?

3. **Plan** — What is my purpose for the reading, writing, listening, or speaking task? Is it to learn, to inform, to entertain, or to persuade? How will I begin? How will I end?

4. **Self-Check** — When I finish, do I understand? What is difficult? Why? Do I need more information? Should I re-read or re-write my work? What did I learn?

Cognitive Strategies — What is the best way to remember?

1. **Use Prior Knowledge** — What do I already know about this topic? Are there things in my home language and culture that can help me learn this new material?

2. **Take Notes** — Did I take notes to remember? Make an outline? Make a timeline?

3. **Make a Visual** — Can I draw a picture to help me understand? Make a chart? Use a graphic organizer?

4. **Make Inferences** — What clues can I use to predict what will happen next?

5. **Summarize** — What is the most important idea?

6. **Use or Make Rules** — Can I see a rule in what I am learning?

7. **Use Mental Images** — Can I make a picture in my mind of what is happening?

8. **Resourcing** — Where can I go to find out information? To a dictionary? To the library? To the Internet? To a classmate? To my teacher? To another adult?

Learning Strategies

Do I work with others to help me learn?

1. **Ask Questions** Who and what can I ask to help me better understand?

2. **Work with Others** How can my classmates help me learn? Can they give me feedback to improve my work? How can I help them?

3. **Positive Self-Talk** I can succeed. I am not afraid to try. Mistakes can help me learn. I need to practice. I can use my new skills outside of class. Learning can be interesting and fun.

Grammar Reference

Nouns

Nouns name a person, place, or thing. Every sentence has a noun.

People	Places	Things
teacher	home	clock

Singular Nouns:
Singular nouns are nouns that name one person, place, or thing.

Plural Nouns:
Plural nouns are nouns that name more than one person, place, or thing.

Spelling Plural Nouns:

Singular	Plural	Rule
fork egg	forks eggs	most nouns: add -s
sandwich potato	sandwiches potatoes	nouns that end in *s, ch, sh, x,* or *consonant + vowel:* add -es
cherry family	cherries families	nouns that end in *consonant + y:* change *y* to *i* and add -es

Irregular Plural Nouns:
Some nouns are irregular in the plural form.

child **children**   foot **feet**   woman **women**
fish **fish**   man **men**

Possessive Nouns:
A possessive noun tells who owns or has something.
Possessive nouns usually end in *'s.*

> ***Yang's*** sister walks to school with him.
> (Yang has a sister. She walks to school with him.)

Pronouns

A **pronoun** takes the place of a noun or refers to a noun.

Subject Pronouns:
Subject pronouns tell who something is about. Subject pronouns are used mostly as the subject of a sentence.

Subject Pronouns
I am a student.
You are a secretary.
He is from Mexico.
She is 15.
It is here.
We are students.
They are in the library.

Object Pronouns
Object pronouns come after a verb or preposition. They show who something happened to, or who got something.

Object Pronouns
You like **me.**
I like **you.**
I like **him.**
I like **her.**
I like **it.**
He likes **us.**
I like **them.**

Possessive Pronouns:
Possessive pronouns tell who owns or has something.

Possessive Pronouns
That book is **mine.**
That book is **yours.**
That book is **his.**
That book is **hers.**
That book is **ours.**
That book is **theirs.**

Grammar Reference

Verbs

A **verb** is an action word. Every sentence has a verb.

Simple Present of *be:*
Be is a verb. Use the simple present of *be* to give information about something happening or true now.

Contractions with the simple present of *be* are: *I'm, you're, he's, she's, it's, we're, they're.*

Simple Present of *be*		
I	**am**	a student.
You	**are**	tall.
He	**is**	my brother.
She	**is**	17.
It	**is**	heavy.
We	**are**	friends.
They	**are**	sisters.

Past Tense of *be:*
Use the past tense of *be* to give information about something that happened or was true in the past.

Past Tense of *be*		
I	**was**	sick yesterday.
You	**were**	sick yesterday.
He	**was**	sick yesterday.
She	**was**	sick yesterday.
It	**was**	sick yesterday.
We	**were**	sick yesterday.
They	**were**	sick yesterday.

Simple Present:
Use the simple present of a verb to tell about an action that usually happens or is happening now. With *he, she,* and *it,* put an *s* after the verb.

Simple Present	
I	**read.**
You	**read.**
He	**reads.**
She	**reads.**
It	**reads.**
We	**read.**
They	**read.**

Grammar Reference

Present Continuous:
The present continuous form of a verb tells about an action happening right now. The present continuous uses *am, is,* or *are* and a main verb. You add *-ing* to the end of the verb.

Present Continuous		
I	**am**	read**ing.**
You	**are**	read**ing.**
He	**is**	read**ing.**
She	**is**	read**ing.**
It	**is**	read**ing.**
We	**are**	read**ing.**
They	**are**	read**ing.**

Past Tense:
The past tense of a verb tells about an action that happened in the past. The past tense of a regular verb ends with *-ed.* Irregular verbs have special forms. See page 199.

Past Tense		
I	work**ed**	yesterday.
You	studi**ed**	yesterday.
He	cook**ed**	yesterday.
She	exercis**ed**	yesterday.
It	play**ed**	yesterday.
We	danc**ed**	yesterday.
They	paint**ed**	yesterday.

Future Tense:
The future tense of a verb tells about an action that will happen in the future. One way of showing the future tense is to use *will* in front of another verb.

Contractions in the future tense using *will* are: *I'll, you'll, he'll, she'll, it'll, we'll, they'll.*

Future Tense		
I	**will**	go.
You	**will**	go.
He	**will**	go.
She	**will**	go.
It	**will**	go.
We	**will**	go.
They	**will**	go.

Grammar Reference

Irregular Verbs

Some verbs are irregular. These verbs do not have *-ed* added to the end in the past tense. They have special past tense forms.

Present	Past
be	was, were
become	became
begin	began
break	broke
bring	brought
buy	bought
come	came
cost	cost
cut	cut
do	did
drink	drank
drive	drove
eat	ate
fall	fell
feel	felt
find	found
fly	flew
get	got
give	gave
go	went
have	had
know	knew

Present	Past
leave	left
make	made
meet	met
pay	paid
put	put
read	read
run	ran
say	said
see	saw
sell	sold
send	sent
sit	sat
sleep	slept
speak	spoke
spend	spent
stand	stood
take	took
teach	taught
tell	told
think	thought
wear	wore
write	wrote

Glossary

A

across from Ch. D
activities Ch. 3
address Ch. 1
after Ch. 8
always Ch. 3
AM Ch. 5
apartment Ch. 4
apartment
  building Ch. 4
April Ch. 1
arm Ch. C
artist Ch. 8
astronaut Ch. 8
ATM card Ch. 7
August Ch. 1

B

backpack Ch. B
bacon Ch. 6
barbecue Ch. 9
baseball Ch. 3
bat Ch. 3
bathroom Ch. 4
bathtub Ch. 4
beans Ch. 6
beautiful Ch. 2
bed Ch. 4
bedroom Ch. 4
bills Ch. 7
bird Ch. 2
black Ch. B
blond Ch. 2
blue Ch. B
blush Ch. 10
board Ch. B
body Ch. C
book Ch. B
bookcase Ch. 4, Ch. D

bookshelf Ch. D
bored Ch. 10
bottom Ch. 6
bowl Ch. 6
boy Ch. A
breakfast Ch. 6
brother Ch. 2
brown Ch. B
bulletin board Ch. D
bus Ch. 5

C

cafeteria Ch. D
calendar Ch. 1
car Ch. 5
card Ch. 9
carpenter Ch. 8
cash Ch. 7
cashier Ch. 8
cat Ch. 2
cereal Ch. 6
chair Ch. B
character Ch. 7
cheap Ch. 7
check Ch. 7
cheek Ch. C
chef Ch. 8
chicken Ch. 6
child-care
  worker Ch. 8
chin Ch. C
chocolates Ch. 9
classmate Ch. C
classroom Ch. B
clay Ch. 8
clock Ch. B
closet Ch. 4
coins Ch. 7
Columbus Day Ch. 9

community Ch. 5
community
  center Ch. 5
computer Ch. B
copy machine Ch. 1
country Ch. B
credit card Ch. 7
cry Ch. 10
curly Ch. 2
curtain Ch. 4
customer Ch. 7

D

dance Ch. 3
date Ch. 1
day Ch. 1
December Ch. 1
desk Ch. B
diet Ch. 6
dime Ch. 7
dinner Ch. 6
doctor Ch. 8
dog Ch. 2
dollar Ch. 7
door Ch. B
dresser Ch. 4
drive Ch. 5
drums Ch. 3

E

ear Ch. C
Earth Day Ch. 9
eggs Ch. 6
eight Ch. B
eighteen Ch. C
eighteenth Ch. 1
eighth Ch. 1
elbow Ch. C
eleven Ch. C

eleventh Ch. 1
embarrassed Ch. 10
eraser Ch. B
excited Ch. 10
exercise Ch. 3
expensive Ch. 7
eye Ch. C

F

face Ch. C
family Ch. 2
father Ch. 2
Father's Day Ch. 9
February Ch. 1
feelings Ch. 10
fifteen Ch. C
fifteenth Ch. 1
fifth Ch. 1
finally Ch. 8
fingers Ch. C
fire station Ch. 5
firefighter Ch. 8
fireworks Ch. 9
first Ch. 1, Ch. 8
five Ch. B
flag Ch. B
flowers Ch. 9
flute Ch. 8
food Ch. 6
foot Ch. C
football Ch. 3
fork Ch. 6
four Ch. B
fourteen Ch. C
fourteenth Ch. 1
fourth Ch. 1
Friday Ch. 1
friend Ch. C

Glossary

G

girl Ch. A
glass Ch. 6
grandfather Ch. 2
grandmother Ch. 2
gray Ch. 2
green Ch. B
grocery store
 clerk Ch. 8
guardian Ch. 1
guitar Ch. 3
gym Ch. D

H

hair Ch. C
hairstylist Ch. 8
hall Ch. D
Halloween Ch. 9
hamburger Ch. 6
hammer Ch. 8
hand Ch. C
handsome Ch. 2
happy Ch. 10
hat Ch. C
head Ch. C
heart Ch. 9
heavy Ch. 2
height Ch. 2
holiday Ch. 9
home Ch. 4
hospital Ch. 5
house Ch. 4

I

Independence Day
 (Fourth of July) Ch. 9
inside Ch. D

J

jacket Ch. C
January Ch. 1
jeans Ch. C
job Ch. 8
jog Ch. 3
July Ch. 1
jump Ch. 10
June Ch. 1

K

keyboard Ch. 1
kitchen Ch. 4
knee Ch. C
knife Ch. 6

L

lamp Ch. 4
laugh Ch. 10
leg Ch. C
length Ch. 2
librarian Ch. D
library Ch. D, Ch. 5
lips Ch. C
living room Ch. 4
locker Ch. D
long Ch. 2
lunch Ch. 6

M

mad Ch. 10
mall Ch. 5
man Ch. A
March Ch. 1
marker Ch. B
Martin Luther King
 Jr. Day Ch. 9
May Ch. 1
mechanic Ch. 8

middle Ch. 6
midnight Ch. 5
mine Ch. D
mirror Ch. 4
Miss Ch. A
Monday Ch. 1
money Ch. 7
month Ch. 1
mother Ch. 2
Mother's Day Ch. 9
mouse Ch. 1
mouth Ch. C
movie theater Ch. 5
Mr. Ch. A
Mrs. Ch. A
Ms. Ch. A
musician Ch. 8
my Ch. D

N

nail Ch. 8
napkin Ch. 6
nationality Ch. B
neck Ch. C
never Ch. 3
New Year's
 Day Ch. 9
next Ch. 8
next to Ch. D
nickel Ch. 7
nine Ch. B
nineteen Ch. C
nineteenth Ch. 1
ninth Ch. 1
noon Ch. 5
nose Ch. C
notebook Ch. B
November Ch. 1

O

October Ch. 1
on the left Ch. D
on the right Ch. D
one Ch. B
orange Ch. B
outside Ch. D
oven Ch. 4

P

paint Ch. 3
paintbrush Ch. 3
paper Ch. 3
parade Ch. 9
parent Ch. 1
park Ch. 5
peas Ch. 6
pen Ch. B
pencil Ch. B
penny Ch. 7
period Ch. C
phone number Ch. 1
pie Ch. 9
pillow Ch. 4
pink Ch. B
pizza Ch. 6
plate Ch. 6
play a sport Ch. 3
play an
 instrument Ch. 3
PM Ch. 5
police station Ch. 5
post office Ch. 5
potatoes Ch. 6
Presidents'
 Day Ch. 9
price Ch. 7
printer Ch. 1
purple Ch. B

Glossary

Q

quarter Ch. 7
question Ch. C
question mark Ch. C

R

read Ch. 3
red Ch. B
refrigerator Ch. 4
rent a video Ch. 3
restaurant Ch. 5
rice Ch. 6
roller skate Ch. 3
roller skates Ch. 3
rug Ch. 4

S

sad Ch. 10
salad Ch. 6
salesperson Ch. 7
sandwich Ch. 6
Saturday Ch. 1
scales Ch. 8
scared Ch. 10
school Ch. A
scissors Ch. 8
screen Ch. 1
second Ch. 1
secretary Ch. 1
sentence Ch. C
September Ch. 1
seven Ch. B
seventeen Ch. C
seventeenth Ch. 1
shake Ch. 10
shirt Ch. C
shoes Ch. C
shop Ch. 3
short Ch. 2

shout Ch. 10
shower Ch. 4
shy Ch. 10
sink Ch. 4
sister Ch. 2
six Ch. B
sixteen Ch. C
sixteenth Ch. 1
sixth Ch. 1
skirt Ch. C
smile Ch. 10
sneakers Ch. C
soccer Ch. 3
sofa Ch. 4
sometimes Ch. 3
soup Ch. 6
spoon Ch. 6
square Ch. B
stairs Ch. D
stapler Ch. 1
steak Ch. 6
stomach Ch. C
straight Ch. 2
student Ch. A
stuffing Ch. 9
Sunday Ch. 1
supermarket Ch. 5
surprised Ch. 10
sweater Ch. C
swim Ch. 3

T

table Ch. 4
tablecloth Ch. 6
tall Ch. 2
teacher Ch. A
teeth Ch. C
telephone Ch. 1
ten Ch. B
tenth Ch. 1
Thanksgiving Ch. 9
then Ch. 8
thermometer Ch. 8
thin Ch. 2
third Ch. 1
thirteen Ch. C
thirteenth Ch. 1
three Ch. B
Thursday Ch. 1
time Ch. 5
toast Ch. 6
toilet Ch. 4
top Ch. 6
train Ch. 5
tray Ch. 8
Tuesday Ch. 1
turkey Ch. 9
twelfth Ch. 1
twelve Ch. C
twentieth Ch. 1
twenty Ch. C
two Ch. B

U

usually Ch. 3

V

Valentine's
  Day Ch. 9
video store Ch. 5

W

waiter Ch. 8
walk Ch. 5
wavy Ch. 2
Wednesday Ch. 1
week Ch. 1
weight Ch. 2
what Ch. 5
when Ch. 5
where Ch. 5
white Ch. B
who Ch. 5
why Ch. 5
window Ch. B
woman Ch. A
work Ch. 3
wrench Ch. 8
write e-mail Ch. 3

Y

yawn Ch. 10
year Ch. 1
yellow Ch. B
your Ch. D
yours Ch. D

Z

zip code Ch. 1

Skills Index

Skills Index

Skills Index

Skills Index

Skills Index

role-play, 87
visually illustrate, 87, 143, 171; AB/1, 2
Pre-reading
graphic organizers, 85, 99, 113, 127, 141, 155, 169
Purposes
complete forms, 58; AB/24
models for writing, 58, 60, 74, 88, 102, 116, 130, 144, 158, 172, 186, 190
Reading Strategies
build background, 57, 71, 85, 99, 113, 127, 141, 155, 169, 183
chronology, 87, 143
compare and contrast, 129, 185; AB/109
compare with own experience, 185
main idea and details, AB/85, 110
outline information, AB/69
predict, 99, 101
preview pictures, 85, 99
prior knowledge, 57, 71, 85, 99, 113, 127, 141, 151, 169, 183
read aloud, AB/46, 94, 102
scan, 59, 115
References
dictionary, 71, 154
Shared Reading, 73, 84, 168; AB/102
Text Sources
anthology, 135
biography, 170
classic work, 142
contemporary work, 100
informational text, 58, 59, 128, 156; AB/37, 45, 61, 69, 77, 85, 93, 101, 109
newspaper, 114
poetry, 23, 72, 84, 86, 124, 152, 168, 184; AB/46, 94, 102
Vocabulary Development
adjectives, 23, 55, 62, 67, 68, 72, 73, 76, 77, 139, 146, 147, 178, 179, 180, 188, 189; AB/41, 48, 82, 83
adverbs of frequency, 81, 82, 90
affixes, 140, 146, 147, 154, 160, 161; AB/84, 92
analogies, 101
assessment, 63, 77, 91, 105, 119, 133, 147, 161, 175, 189
authentic literature, 23, 54, 84, 110, 124, 140, 152; AB/37, 45, 53, 61, 69, 77, 85, 93, 101, 109
compound words, 98, 104, 105, 107; AB/60, Mini-Reader Ch. 4
content area words, 58, 72, 86, 100, 114, 128, 142, 156, 170, 184; AB/16, 32, 37, 45, 53, 61, 69, 77, 85, 93, 101, 109
contractions, 26, 45, 69; AB/12, 43, 51, 67, 98, 99, 106, 107
derivatives, 98, 104, 105, 140
listening to selections, 72, 86
review, 62, 76, 90, 104, 118, 132, 146, 160, 174, 188; AB/53, 69, 77, 85, 93, 101, 109
root words, 140, 154
sight vocabulary, 2–3, 7, 13, 14–15, 19, 23, 27, 28–29, 33, 40–41, 44, 45, 49, 50, 52, 54, 62, 63, 66, 67, 68, 76, 77, 80, 81, 82, 90, 91, 94, 95, 96, 104, 105, 108, 109, 110, 118, 119, 122, 124, 132, 133, 136, 138, 139, 146, 147, 150, 151, 152, 160, 161, 164, 165, 166, 174, 175, 178, 179, 180, 188, 189, 192; AB/16, 17, 22, 24, 27, 32, 37, 45, 48, 49, 53, 57, 61, 69, 70, 73, 74, 77, 85, 93, 97, 101, 105, 109
simile, 101
time words, 110, 118; AB/65, 71, 72, 79, 96
word origins, 98, 104, 105, 140
Word Identification, AB/13
assess, 63, 77, 91, 105, 119, 133, 147, 161, 175, 189
derivations, 98, 104, 105, 140
dictionary, 71, 74, 93, 95, 123, 151, 154, 179
letter-sound correspondences, 4–5, 8–9, 16–17, 20–21, 30–31, 34–35, 42–43, 46–47, 56, 62, 63, 70, 73, 76, 77, 84, 90, 112, 168, 182, 188; AB/13, 21, 29, 36,

44, 68, 76, 100, 108
meanings, 140, 154; AB/84
prefixes, 140, 146, 147; AB/84, Mini-Reader Ch. 7
pronunciation, 13, 27, 39, 51, 56, 62, 63, 70, 73, 76, 77, 84, 90, 112, 126; AB/76
review, 62, 76, 90, 104, 118, 132, 146, 160, 174, 188; AB/53, 69, 77, 85, 93, 101, 109
root words, 140, 154
suffixes, 154, 160, 161; AB/92, Mini-Reader Ch. 8
word-picture correspondences, 92, 96, 98, 104, 106, 137, 154; AB/9, 25, 60, 65, 97, 105
word search, AB/17, 57

Viewing and Representing

Analysis
interpret and evaluate meaning, 38, 101; AB/82
visual media, 56, 85, 101; AB/32, 37, 53, 61, 65, 69, 82
respond to media, 101, 115
visuals, 56, 85; AB/32, 37, 53, 61, 65, 69, 82
Illustrations
posters, 106, 134, 176
sequence of events, 87, 143, 157, 163, 171, 172; AB/1
store inventory and prices, 148, 149
to support written text, 101, 103, 107, 121, 159, 169, 171, 173; AB/37, 53, 61, 69, 77, 85, 93, 101, 109
to tell story, 74, 78, 92, 93, 103, 121, 177
Interpretation
color, 26, 68; AB/15
important events, 171, 172, 190; AB/37, 104
important ideas, 38; AB/45, 53
line, AB/1, 2, 8, 9, 11, 25, 87
shape, 23; AB/3
Media
graphic art, AB/65
print, AB/37, 65
Production
charts, 56, 82, 99, 115, 125, 152, 169; AB/33, 57, 72, 80, 88, 97
media, 148
technology, 75
visuals, 67, 68, 159, 171, 177
communication, 106, 121, 134, 163, 176
menu, 148
own story, 74, 78, 92, 93, 103; AB/73
store inventory and prices, 148, 149
Respond to Media
support opinions, 101, 115

Vocabulary and Language

Actions, 80–81, 83, 90, 91; AB/49
Activities, 80, 81, 82, 85, 90, 164, 165, 166, 174, 175; AB/49, 56, 61, Mini-Reader Ch. 3
Address, 60–61; AB/39, 40, 61
Adjectives, 33, 55, 62, 67, 68, 72, 73, 74, 75, 76, 77, 78, 139, 146, 147, 178, 179, 180, 188, 189; AB/41, 48, 82, 83
Age, 32, 37, 59
Animals, 66, 76; AB/41
Ask for Information, 6, 18, 32, 33, 45, 50, 53, 67, 81, 95, 109, 123, 138; AB/Mini-Reader Ch. 1
Assessment, 63, 77, 91, 105, 119, 133, 147, 161, 175, 189
Body Parts, 33, 39; AB/22
Calendar, 54, 65; AB/33
Classroom, 14–15, 27, 49, 51; AB/9, 16, 30
Clock, 110; AB/65

Skills Index

Clothing, 28–29, 39; AB/17, 24
Colors, 23, 26, 27, 36–37, 50, 68; AB/15, 17, 24
Community, 23, 108, 109, 118, 119; AB/65, 69, Mini-Reader Ch. 5
Compare, 101, 139, 146, 147; AB/82, 83
Content Areas
  arts, AB/53
  language arts, 58, 72, 86, 100, 114, 128, 142, 156, 170, 184
  math, AB/16
  science, AB/45, 93, 109
  social studies, AB/32, 37, 61, 69, 77, 85, 101
Countries, 18–19, 23, 27, 32; AB/11, 12, 77, 85
Dates, AB/39, 40, 61, 71, 72
Days of the Week, 54, 62, 63; AB/33, 47
Description Words
  eye color, 33, 36–37, 72; AB/23, 48, Mini-Reader Ch. 2
  hair, 33, 36–37, 68, 72; AB/23, 41, 48, Mini-Reader Ch. 2
  height, 68; AB/41, 48, Mini-Reader Ch. 2
  weight, 68; AB/41, 48, Mini-Reader Ch. 2
Directions, 44, 45, 49, 51, 109; AB/32
Family, 66, 67, 76; AB/41
Feelings, 85, 178, 179, 180, 184, 188, 189; AB/105, Mini-Reader Ch. 10
Food, 122, 124, 132, 133, 176; AB/73, 74, 77, Mini-Reader Ch. 6
Frequently-Used Words, 192
Give Information, 6, 18, 32, 33, 45, 50, 53, 67, 81, 95, 109, 123, 138; AB/Mini-Reader Ch. 1
Greetings, 6–7, 12, 13, 18–19, 22, 32–33, 53, 186, 190; AB/7, 8, 12, 19, 30, 33, 47
Holidays, 164, 166, 174, 175; AB/37, 97, Mini-Reader Ch. 9
Home, 66, 94, 96; AB/57, Mini-Reader Ch. 4
Introductions, 6–7, 12, 13, 18–19, 22, 32, 33, 45, 49; AB/12, 19
Jobs, 49, 150, 151, 160, 161, 162; AB/89, Mini-Reader Ch. 8
Meals, 122, 123, 127, 128–129; AB/73, 74, Mini-Reader Ch. 6
Money, 136, 138, 139, 146, 147, 149; AB/81, 85, Mini-Reader Ch. 7
Months of the Year, 54, 60, 62, 63; AB/47
Nationality, 18–19, 23, 27, 32; AB/12, 19, 47
Numbers
  cardinal, 23, 24–25, 27, 32, 39; AB/14, 16, 20
  in dates, phone numbers or addresses, 60; AB/39, 40, 61, 71, 72
  monetary amounts, 136, 146, 147, 149; AB/81, 85
  ordinal, 54, 62; AB/96
Objects
  arts, 82, 90; AB/53
  classroom, 14–15, 27, 40–41, 51, 52; AB/9, 25, 31
  flag, 23
  home, 66, 76, 94, 96, 124; AB/57, 73
  job, 49, 52, 62, 152, 160, 161, 163; AB/89
  sports, 82, 90
  table settings, 124, 132, 133
Pay, Ways to, 137, 138; AB/81
People, 2–3, 13, 49, 52, 66, 67, 76, 150, 151; AB/23, 30, 41, 47
Personal Information, 6–7, 12, 13, 18–19, 22, 32, 33, 45, 58, 59, 69, 81; AB/39, 40, 47, 48
Places, 18–19, 44, 45, 49, 51; AB/32, 47, 65, 71, 72
Prices, 137, 146, 147, 148, 149; AB/24, Mini-Reader Ch. 7
Quantity Words
  count and noncount, 125, 126, 131, 132, 133; AB/74, 75, 76, 80, Mini-Reader Ch. 6
  money, AB/81, 85
Question Words, 6, 12, 13, 18–19, 26, 27, 32, 33, 37, 38, 45, 67, 81, 95, 109, 114, 116, 118, 120, 121, 123; AB/104
Review, 62, 76, 90, 104, 118, 132, 146, 160, 174, 188; AB/53, 69, 77, 85, 93, 101, 109

Rooms, 14–15, 40–41, 44, 51, 52; AB/25, 30, 57, Mini-Reader Ch. 4
School
  classroom objects, 14–15, 27, 40–41, 51, 52; AB/9, 25, 31, 33
  locations, 14–15, 40–41, 44, 49, 52; AB/25, 27, 30
  subjects, AB/16
School Office, 49, 52, 53; AB/27, 30, 33
Sequence Words, 158–159, 160, 163; AB/96
Shapes, 23; AB/3
Sight Words, 102, 192; AB/70
Sports, 80, 81, 82; AB/49
Table Settings, 124, 132, 133; AB/73
Telling Time, 110, 118; AB/65
Time Words, 110, 118; AB/65, 71, 72, 79, 96
Tools, 152; AB/89
Transportation, 108, 109, 118; AB/Mini-Reader Ch. 5

Writing

Addresses, 60–61
Affixes, AB/84, 92
Alphabet, 4–5, 8, 10, 13; AB/4, 5, 6, 10, 18, 21, 26, 29
Auxiliary Verbs, 181
Capitalization
  first letter in sentence, 37, 75, 89, 103; AB/11, 12, 23, 47, 48, 56, 64, 87
  names, AB/11, 12, 23, 39, 40, 47
Connections
  authors, 100
  collaboration with other writers, 64, 65, 79, 92, 121, 134, 148
  correspondence
    mail, 162, 186
Contractions, 26, 45, 69; AB/12, 43, 51, 67, 98, 99, 106, 107
Dates
  arrange into correct phrase, AB/71, 72
  numbers in, AB/39, 40, 61
Drafts
  blend paragraphs, AB/111, 112
  organize ideas, 74, 88, 103, 116, 121, 130, 144, 158, 172, 186; AB/48, 56, 64, 72, 80, 88, 104, 112
  organize paragraphs, 173; AB/111, 112
  organize sentences, 88, 103, 117, 131, 145, 159, 173, 187; AB/48, 56, 64, 72, 80, 88, 96, 104
  supporting details, 131, 145; AB/80, 88
  topic sentence, AB/80, 88
Edit Writing, 61, 75, 89, 103, 117, 131, 145, 159, 173, 187; AB/40, 48, 56, 64, 72, 80, 88, 96, 104, 112
  subject-verb agreement, 103; AB/64
  verb tenses, 75, 103, 167, 173; AB/48, 56, 64, 104
Forms
  autobiography, 172–173; AB/112
  biography, 177; AB/104
  class birthday book, 64
  class calendar, 65
  class how-to book, 159
  class recipe book, 135
  collage, 92
  description
    activities, AB/56
    community event, AB/72
    eating habits, AB/80
    family member, AB/41
    house or apartment, AB/64

Skills Index

Credits

Text Credits

p. 72, BABY BROTHER. From FATHERS, MOTHERS, SISTERS, BROTHERS: A COLLECTION OF FAMILY POEMS by Mary Ann Hoberman. Copyright © 1991 by Mary Ann Hoberman (Text); copyright © 1991 by Marylin Hafner (illustrations). By permission of Little, Brown and Company (Inc.). Audio recorded by permission of Gina Maccoby Literary Agency.

p. 86, 74th STREET. From MAILBU AND OTHER POEMS by Myra Cohn Livingston. Copyright © 1972 Myra Cohn Livingston. Used by permission of Marian Reiner.

p. 100, A HOUSE OF MY OWN. From THE HOUSE ON MANGO STREET. Copyright © 1984 by Sandra Cisneros. Published by Vintage Books, a division of Random House, Inc., and in hardcover by Alfred A. Knopf in 1994. Reprinted by permission of Susan Bergholz Literary Services, New York. All rights reserved.

p. 111, A CIRCLE OF SUN. Text copyright © 1998 by Rebecca Kai Dotlich from LEMONADE SUN AND OTHER SUMMER POEMS written by Rebecca Kai Dotlich, illustrated by Jan Spivey Gilchrist. Published by Wordsong, Boyds Mills Press, Inc. Reprinted by permission.

p. 124, HOW TO EAT A POEM. From JAMBOREE RHYMES FOR ALL TIMES by Eve Merriam. Copyright © 1962, 1964, 1966, 1973, 1984 by Eve Merriam. All rights renewed and reserved. Used by permission of Marian Reiner.

p. 168, FOURTH OF JULY NIGHT. From POETRY PLACE ANTHOLOGY by Eleanor Dennis. Copyright © 1983 by Eleanor Dennis. Reprinted by permission of Scholastic, Inc.

p. 184, PATTI BENNET. "Patti Bennet," from THE TAKING OF ROOM 114 by Mel Glenn, copyright © 1997 by Mel Glenn. Used by permission of Lodestar Books, an affiliate of Dutton Children's Books, an imprint of Penguin Putnam Books for Young Readers, a division of Penguin Putnam, Inc. All rights reserved.

Illustrators

Catherine Duffy: pp. 65, 92, 106, 134, 135, 149, 157 (Catherine Duffy/Publicom); **Rich McMahon:** pp. 6, 8, 19, 23, 30, 44, 45, 67, 68, 74, 79, 82, 95, 96, 104, 110, 114, 116, 121, 124, 125, 127, 137, 138, 139, 139, 142, 148, 152, 166, 168, 176, 179, 180, 183, 190 (Rich McMahon/Publicom); **Tim Jones:** pp. 38, 50, 86, 87, 100, 140 (Tim Jones/Wilkinson Studios).

Photos

Cartesia: p. 4 *map* (© Cartesia)

Cheryl Clegg Photography: pp. 2–3, 4 *tl, tr, c;* 5 *tc, tr;* 6 *all;* 7 *tl, tr, brc, bl;* 11, 14–15, 16 *tc, tr; 5:5;* 17 *tc, 8:1;* 18 *all;* 22 *cr, cl, bc, c;* 28–28; 30 *4:1, 4:8;* 32 *all;* 37, 40 *br, tr, bl;* 45 *all;* 49 *all;* 52, 59, 75, 78, 80 *ct;* 89, 93, 107 *all;* 163, 178 *cr, bc, bl, c, cl, tr, tl;* 184, 191 (Cheryl Clegg Photography).

Comstock: 4 *bl;* 5 *brc;* 16 *5:3;* 42 *tr;* 46 *13:5;* 67 *br;* 96 *6a, 6b, 6d, 6c;* 98 *11e;* 141 *l;* 154 *l* (© Comstock Images).

Corbis: p. 5 *br* (© Philippa Lewis; Edifice/Corbis), p. 11 *22:7* (© Philippa Lewis; Edifice/Corbis), p. 42 *5:6, 4:6* (© Craig Tuttle/Corbis), p. 71 (© Larry Williams/Corbis), p. 99 (© Gail Mooney/Corbis), p. 105 *c* (© Elizabeth Hathon/Corbis), p. 108 *tl* (© Bob Rowan; Progressive Image/Corbis), p. 108 *bcl* (Royalty-Free/Corbis), p. 108 *cl* (© William A. Baker/Corbis), p. 113 *c* (© Chris Jones/Corbis), p. 113 *l* (© Kelly-Mooney Photography/Corbis), p. 114 *b* (© Mug Shots/Corbis), p. 122 *chicken* (Royalty-Free/Corbis), p. 150 *cl*

(© Jim Zuckerman/Corbis), p. 150 *bl* (© Jose Luis Pelaez, Inc./Corbis), p. 156 (© Baldev/Corbis Sygma), p. 169 (© Steve Raymer/Corbis), p. 170 (© Corbis Kipa), p. 177 *l, r* (© Bettmann/Corbis).

Dan Walsh Photography: pp. 4 *br;* 9 *17:6;* 16 *4:8;* 17 *tl;* 20 *tr;* 24 *24:7;* 26 *24:9, 28:4, 28:5;* 30 *tcl, 5:6;* 31 *7:2;* 42 *tl;* 43 *8:3;* 66 *trc;* 98 *11a, 11d;* 105 *l;* 112 *10:1;* 136 *money;* 137 *money;* 138 *tl* (Dan Walsh Photography).

Getty Images Royalty Free: pp. 4 *tc, bc, cr;* 5 *tl, bl, bc, bl, bl;* 7 *blc, br;* 9 *br, 17:5;* 16 *tl, 5:1, 5:6, 5:2;* 17 *tr, 7:5, 8:2, 8:3, 8:6;* 24 *24:5;* 26 *24:3, 28:6;* 30 *tl, 5:2, 5:4, 4:6, 5:1;* 31 *tl, tr;* 33 *l, r;* 34 *bl, br;* 36, 42 *tc, 5:3, 4:5 5:1;* 43 *7:2, 8:6, 8:1, 7:8;* 53 *br;* 56 *11:3, 11:9, 11:6;* 57, 66 *tl, tr, tlc;* 67 *bl;* 72, 77 *br;* 80 *cr;* 82 *5:7, 7:2, 5:3, 5:5, 5:10, 7:3, 7:5;* 85, 94 *cl;* 98 *11b, 11c, 11f;* 108 *cbr, cr, bcr, bl;* 112 *10:3, 10:4, 10:5;* 114 *c;* 122 *tr, eggs, toast, lunch;* 125 *8:2, 8:3, 8:4, 8:5, 8:6;* 136 *background;* 141 *c, r;* 154 *r; c,* 155 *l;* 164 *cl, l, t;* 165, 178 *br, bc inset;* 182 *10:8, 10:7* (© PhotoDisc/GettyImages), pp. 127, 150 *tl* (© Eyewire/GettyImages).

Getty Images Creative: p. 46 *13:2* (© Josef Fankhauser/The Image Bank/GettyImages), p. 47 *15:5* (© Josef Fankhauser/The Image Bank/GettyImages), p. 66 *b* (© Dick Luria/Taxi/GettyImages), p. 122 *bkgrnd.* (© FoodPix/GettyImages), p. 128 (© John Kelly/Stone/GettyImages), p. 138 *tc* (© Larry Bray/Taxi/GettyImages).

Heinle: pp. 30 *5:3;* 40 *tl;* 67 *tr;* 80 *tr;* 80 *br;* 82 *5:1, 5:2, 5:4, 5:6;* 105 *r;* 122 *rice* (Heinle).

Index Stock Photography: p. 5 *blc* (© Dan Gair Photographic/Index Stock Imagery), p. 5 *bcc* (© PUSH/Index Stock Imagery), p. 9 *17:3, 18:1* (© PUSH/Index Stock Imagery), p. 11 *22:4* (© PUSH/Index Stock Imagery), p. 17 *7:3* (© Index Stock Imagery), p. 20 *br* (© Chad Ehlers/Index Stock Imagery), p. 34 *tl* (© Benelux Press/Index Stock Imagery), p. 35 *18:1* (© Benelux Press/Index Stock Imagery), p. 42 *5:4, 4:8* (© Index Stock Imagery), p. 42 *4:3* (© Len Delessio/Index Stock Imagery), p. 46 *13:4* (© Gary Conner/Index Stock Imagery), p. 47 *15:1* (© Gary Conner/Index Stock Imagery), p. 80 *tl* (© Alyx Kellington/Index Stock Imagery), p. 80 *bc* (© Bonnie Kamin/Index Stock Imagery), p. 80 *bl* (© Bonnie Kamin/Index Stock Imagery), p. 80 *bl* (© Grantpix/Index Stock Imagery), p. 80 *cb* (© SW Production/Index Stock Imagery), p. 82 *5:9* (© D2 Productions/Index Stock Imagery), p. 94 *cr* (© Erin Garvey/Index Stock Imagery), p. 94 *tl* (© Philip Wegener-Kantor/Index Stock Imagery), p. 94 *bl* (© Philip Wegener-Kantor/Index Stock Imagery), p. 94 *br* (© Silvestre Machado/Index Stock Imagery), p. 94 *tr* (© Wallace Garrison/Index Stock Imagery), p. 108 *tr* (© Aneal Vohra/Index Stock Imagery), p. 108 *br* (© Harvey Schwartz/Index Stock Imagery), p. 108 *c* (© James Lemass/Index Stock Imagery), p. 108 *cbl* (© Jeff Perkell/Index Stock Imagery), p. 113 *r* (© Myrleen Cate/Index Stock Imagery), p. 121 (© Wayne Hoy/Index Stock Imagery), p. 125 *8:1* (© Great American Stock/Index Stock Imagery), p. 154 *br* (© Peter Gregoire/Index Stock), p. 164 *r* (© David Burch/Index Stock Imagery).

NCR Corporation: 155 *r* (NCR Corporation).

PictureQuest: p. 150 *br* (© Andersen-Ross/Brand X Pictures/PictureQuest), p. 150 *c* (© Corbis Images/PictureQuest), p. 150 *tr* (© Creatas/PictureQuest), p. 164 *bl* (© Tony Freeman/PhotoEdit/PictureQuest).

Publicom: p. 31 *tc* (Courtesy, Ruth Rothstein/Publicom).

Superstock: Cover (© Superstock).

U.S. Fish & Wildlife Service: p. 31 *8:3* (James C. Leupold/U.S. Fish and Wildlife Service), p. 43 *7:4* (Gary M. Stolz/U.S. Fish and Wildlife Service).